Youth and leisure in an urban sprawl

Youth and leisure
in an urban sprawl

Isabel Emmett

for the

Department of Physical Education
University of Manchester

Manchester University Press

Manchester at

r M13 9NR

ber: 0 7190 0431 4

Contents

Figures

Preface

In September 1965 the Leverhulme Trust Fund made a grant to the Physical Education Department of Manchester University so that a study could be conducted in the south-east Lancashire conurbation of post-school adolescents' leisure activities, particularly in the field of physical recreation. The study was planned to take place in two stages, the first being based on questions put to a sample of children in their last year at school, and the second being based on interviews with the same children nearly three years later.

This report on the first stage was not written for publication but as a working paper, prepared to satisfy the requirements of the Leverhulme Trust Fund. Since its first limited circulation, however, it has been in demand, and, the small stock of duplicated copies proving inadequate, the decision was made to publish it. Readers should bear in mind that the original intention was to report on the research as a whole. The present document is a purely descriptive account of the first stage of a five-year research project, and was written in 1967.

I.E.

Introduction

This report summarises what has been done in the first stage of a study designed to look at school leavers in their last year at school and nearly three years after they have left school, and to find out as much as possible about the factors which affect the part that physical recreation plays in their lives.

The fifty-two local authorities in the conurbation of south-east Lancashire were listed in order of geographical spread.[1] Underneath the name of each local authority were listed all the secondary modern schools and, in separate lists, all the grammar and technical schools in that area. There were 222 secondary modern schools, 52 grammar and 21 technical schools in all. Every tenth school was chosen, starting with one chosen randomly. Modern schools were stratified by size and grammar schools by sex, and 22 modern, five grammar and two technical schools were thus chosen. One of the three schools at that time known as comprehensive schools was chosen, but in the analysis of results it was grouped with the secondary modern schools, as the presence of grammar schools in the vicinity meant that its intake was not comprehensive. Head teachers were asked if all leavers in these 30 schools could be questioned, and as far as is known all leavers in these schools, apart from those absent on the day of questioning, were questioned. One in three of the absentees have been questioned briefly by post to see if their absence biased the results, but their answers have not yet been analysed. In the 23 direct grant schools in the conurbation, 10 per cent of the leavers in each school were questioned.

The questionnaire was twice piloted and revised, and was administered by members of the Physical Education Department. In each case the author or another member of the team explained to the children why the research was being done, undertook to guarantee the anonymity of the responses, and asked for frank and honest co-operation. Poor writers were

---

[1] The local authorities were listed in order from west to east, starting in the north and proceeding to the south of the conurbation.

given help, slow writers were given time, fast writers were given essays to write while their companions continued completing the forms. Questionnaires that had to be discarded because of frivolity of responses, illegibility, or because they were not completed, numbered five in all, and those working on the research were impressed by the serious and honest response.

A total of 2,685 children completed readable questionnaires in 53 schools in the conurbation. Results will not be ready until answers from the second stage of the enquiry, when the same children were questioned late in 1968 and early in 1969, are analysed, so that the figures and conclusions reported herein are provisional. Some of the hypotheses to be tested were as follows:

1 Boys are more actively interested in sport[2] than girls.
2 Sport-loving youngsters are more commonly found among children of middle class origin than among children of working class origin.
3 Sport-loving youngsters are more commonly found in selective schools than in other schools.
4 Fourteen and 15 year olds are more sport-loving than 16–17 year olds.
5 As opposed to team games, outdoor activities are more commonly taken up by children of middle class origin than by children of working class origin, and by selective school children than by other children.
6 Children from schools which offer varied games and sports will be more likely to continue in the years immediately after leaving school with an active interest in sport than those from other schools.
7 Cutting across class and age is what is here called a 'with it-ness' factor, i.e. commitment to adolescent rather than adult values, and fewer 'with it' youngsters will like sport than will other youngsters.
8 Cutting across class and type of school, and separate from commitment to adolescent or adult values, is a solitary or

[2] 'Sport' in this report is used as a shorthand term for active participation in physical recreation.

home oriented/gregarious factor and solitary or home oriented children will, in their physical activities, be more prone to participate in team games than will gregarious children.

9 Children living in parts of the conurbation relatively well provided with facilities for recreation will be more likely to take an active interest in sport and to continue with such an interest than those from poorly provided districts.

These hypotheses are no more than hunches which sprang from first thoughts about the place of physical recreation in the lives of young people. Some of these first thoughts, or general notions, stemming for the most part from commonplaces in the sociological literature, are spelt out briefly here simply to explain why these and not other hypotheses were looked at, and to make explicit the underlying slant of the study.

When decisions are made about the kind, degree and location of provision which should be made for physical recreation in Great Britain such decisions cannot be made solely on the basis of assumptions about static personality traits in the population. It is not adequate to count the people who say they 'want' tennis courts, assume that each such 'want' is a stable part of each person who expresses it, and on this basis provide tennis courts. 'Wants' are flexible. The existence of tennis courts, their location and amenities will influence an individual's proneness to play tennis. The values of those who provide facilities, and what they think is good, will affect the number of tennis courts in existence and thus the number of people who play tennis. Changes in fashions in sport will influence an individual's proneness to play tennis.

The main media through which an individual is introduced to his initial activity in any field, including sport, are the social groups to which he belongs and these groups are also the vehicle through which changes in fashion affect him. The social groups to which a person belongs are related to the major divisions in our society, such as sex, age, social class, town and country. Statistics collected on most subjects in Great Britain show major variations in these major divisions. This study does not aim at discovering people's 'needs' in the field of physical

3

recreation so much as enquire into the factors which affect the physical recreation in which young people participate.

The assumption is that as changes occur which relate to these factors, so will 'needs' change. Thus sex is a factor which affects the physical recreation in which young people participate. If changes occur in girls' education or in society's expectations of girls' behaviour, then it is probable that girls' participation in sport will change. Social class is a factor which affects the physical recreation in which young people participate. If changes occur in the relationship between social classes and in the education of working class and middle class youths, it is probable that class differences in participation in sport will change.

The first stage of the research was seen primarily as an opportunity to discover the main groupings into which each respondent fell. In the follow-up, when each child was interviewed personally at home, more detailed enquiry was made into his experiences in active sport, and the way he saw the facilities for, and the attractions of, various sports.

Sex and social class

There is a process of socialisation by which children are inculcated with the values of the adult world. This process takes place at home—particularly in early childhood—at school, and at work. The process occurs differently to girls and boys, to middle class and to working class children: adult values are not a coherent whole, taught in the same way to all young people.

The traditional middle class attitude to sport in British society stems from the moral code of public schools and the belief which was part of that code, that participation in sport led to the development of such virtues as selflessness, discipline, clean-mindedness and other respected characteristics. This code was based in part on a notion of what life was like in some ancient Greek city states. The notion that sport was a good thing in this sense spread widely throughout British society, partly because the ethic of the middle class has been the ruling ethic of our time. The ethic taught in school tends to be a middle class ethic. Some parents try to teach a moral code which they themselves do not necessarily live by. Children are sent to Sunday school by parents who never go to church; learn to respect the royal family, be good losers, and amongst many other things learn that sport is a good thing. But this lesson is particularly well learned by children of middle class parents, because their parents are likely to have attended educational establishments modelled on Victorian public schools. The transmission of the message is facilitated by the fact that middle class children spend a great deal of time at home in early childhood, and can communicate relatively easily with their parents because of this, and because of a strong verbal tradition.

Though the ruling ethic is the ethic of the middle class, working class values exist: working class children learn them at home, in the peer group and at work. In this system of values, sport is not conceptualised as a separate entity in the same way as it is for middle class people. But many sports, and watching sport, are approved leisure pursuits: not virtues so much as some of several manly pleasures. As far as attitude to sport is concerned, then, working class values support, inarticulately but definitely, the middle class attitude taught in most schools in the case of boys.

Girls are used more than boys to help in the domestic routine. It is expected that most of a girl's adult role will be performed in a house and therefore she is trained in household tasks. For these and other reasons, girls in our society probably spend more time at home than do boys, over the whole years of childhood, and acquire more of their values from home than do boys. In middle class homes their tuition lays the foundation for what is taught at school. In working class homes, their tuition in many ways runs counter to what is taught at school.

In the past, in both systems of values, sport has been connected with manliness and women have not been thought to be in the same need of an outlet for boisterous spirits as have boys. Active participation in sport by girls was long considered unwomanly in middle class spheres, and a waste of time that could not be afforded in working class spheres. As girls' grammar schools borrowed the ideals of the Victorian public schools in emulation of boys' grammar schools, sport became 'good' for girls in the middle class code, but a similar change did not take place in the working class system of values. Many working

B

women think that they will get enough physical exercise from life's labours without particularly looking for it. Whilst many working class women attend keep fit classes and see in them an aid to beauty and an escape from domestic chores, active physical recreation plays little part in the lives of most working class women. The more recent arguments in favour of active recreation also concentrate on men, who fear the consequences of an increasingly sedentary life. One hears of men spending too much time at desk and steering wheel, and succumbing to coronary thrombosis: it is men who are urged to walk to work.

Thus, quite apart from any individual or physical differences which may exist and account for different attitudes towards sport on the part of young people, school leavers in Britain place a different value on sport, as on many other things, by dint of growing up in working class or middle class environments; as girls or as boys. It was these considerations which led to the hypotheses that boys would be more sport-loving than girls, and that middle class children would be more sport-loving than working class children.

Adult values versus adolescent values

School leavers were chosen as the subject of this study because school leaving is a crisis in the life cycle during which radical changes are thought to occur in the amount and kind of physical recreation pursued. School leaving is a crisis in far more ways than this, and its wide impact must be taken into account.

Adolescents are treated more as a separate section of society at present than has ever been the case. This treatment partly reflects the division between generations which is increasing with the increasing pace of social change. It partly reflects the fact that a section of the commercial world magnifies that division and spreads by national networks of communication the changes in musical taste, dress and speech initiated by young people. This commercial activity in turn reflects the relatively new affluence of adolescents, whose wages, while they are single, are largely available for spending on leisure.

For these and other reasons there has grown up a consciousness on the part of adolescents that they *are* adolescent and belong to a generation which has graduated from most of the

6

restrictions of childhood and is still free from the restrictions of parenthood. The fact that adolescents are treated as a separate section of society and are conscious of themselves as a separate section of society has led to the growth of what has been described variously as a teenage culture, a youth sub-culture, a mass youth culture, an adolescent society.[3] Perhaps sub-culture is the appropriate term: 'society' suggests a fairly structured social entity; 'sub-culture' is more indicative of the pooled set of symbols and values which young people use to a greater or lesser extent. Youth in Britain does not comprise a group; nor does it form a homogeneous section of society.

Individual teenagers rightly resent being treated as part of a porridge-like mass. Teenagers have very varied interests and behave in vary varied ways. Dr Cyril Smith[4] stresses that the overwhelming majority of adolescents go to work and go on to marry, raise children and continue the traditions of the society into which they grow up. However, there is an inter-action between young people in their local streets, in their local cafes and clubs, on the one hand, and entertainers and writers in television and radio programmes, publications and films designed for young people, on the other. This interaction has created a distinctive style of living and speaking which is followed by some teenagers, particularly leaders of opinion, and appeals to many others. The values associated with this distinctive life style are distinctive too—in the sense that the priorities are distinctive. Most members of society agree on what are virtues but to know what is virtuous is not to have a guide to action, since the virtues conflict with each other: the dictates of honesty conflict with the dictates of loyalty; caring for your own children prevents you from giving to the poor. Thus people hold different values to the extent that they have different priorities, and valuing a quality is meaningful only to the extent that they pay the cost of valuing that quality, which is to reject its opposites. Young people value some things more than adults do because they dislike more intensely the vices which spring from the lack of these qualities. The content of adolescent values is not only an affirmation of certain virtues such as

[3] See James S. Coleman, *The Adolescent Society*, New York, Free Press, 1967.
[4] See Cyril S. Smith, *Adolescence*, Harlow, Longmans, 1968.

gaiety, sincerity, personal freedom and novelty but also a rejection of others which have high priority for adults. The particular stress of the teenage sub-culture is upon symbols of adolescents' separateness. It is as though the teenager were saying 'We are going to become spouses, parents, workers, citizens, responsible, 'square'. We agree with you about most things. We don't challenge the structure of society. But until we do become spouses, parents, workers and citizens we are not old; we are young; we are free; we are different.'

It is difficult for a group to have an identity without posing itself against some other group. This is true of political groups, religious groups, nationalities and different generations. British youth is not a group; but it includes groups within it which are very influential, and leaders of opinion in the adolescent sub-culture are anti-adult in this sense : that they require to be anti-adult in order to be separate. The crux of the message is difference. Adults say that sport is one of the things young people should do with their leisure. 'With it' youngsters don't do sport, not only because their sub-culture is associated with other things—with music, dance, dress and conviviality—but also, perhaps, because adults say sport is one of the things young people should do with their leisure.

The teenage term for approaching closely to this distinctive life style is being 'with it', and this term has been adopted for the sake of brevity. It is not practical to look at the leisure pursuits of young people without taking into acount the appeal of the adolescent sub-culture, and it is these considerations which led to the hypothesis that 'with it' youngsters would tend not to be sport-loving.

The notions behind hypothesis 8 are related to the above argument. A young person may have many friends and not be 'with it' : there are other sub-cultures among adolescents than 'the' adolescent sub-culture referred to above. Working class boys may be attached to a street corner gang which is consciously not 'with it'; a particular interest or hobby may lead a sociable person away from the main current of adolescent preoccupations without him ceasing to be gregarious. Similarly a solitary person may be 'with it' all alone, following trends in pop music through television, radio and records; and following trends in clothes by reading magazines or seeing films. Thus the solitary or home oriented/gregarious continuum is not the same as the square/with it continuum, although there is a relationship between them.

Hypothesis 8 suggests that solitary or home-oriented children will, in their physical activities, be more prone to participate in team games than in less organised activities. It is not easy to go bowling, skating or rock climbing completely alone. These are activities which one does casually with friends. The solitary child is more likely, in so far as he or she is interested in sport, to belong to an organisation, to join a team.[5]

The extent to which these and other hypotheses can be said to be tested by an enquiry of this sort is worth considering. No behaviour has been observed. All the data consist of what children in their last year at school wrote down in answer to written questions which they themselves read. Their interest in reading the questions varied, as did their understanding of the words in the questions.

For children who engage in water sports, the distinction between canoeing, sailing, pleasure craft cruising and rowing is important. They know they did row but did not canoe. A question which did not admit the distinction would not be precise enough for them to answer 'yes' to. But for children who do not engage in water sports such distinctions are meaningless, and the child who occasionally goes on the boats in the park may well not know which of the bewildering lists to tick and so tick nothing or everything. One style of wording will be very bad for some children; another will be very bad for others.

The difficulty of varying interpretations of the wording of questions sometimes is related to variations in social class and associated differences in experience and in reading ability. But more complex patterns of variation appear. Thus children were asked first 'If you could have any job you wanted when you left school, or finished full-time education, what job would you choose?' and then 'The world being what it is, what job do

---

[5] For what is meant by 'team sports' in this report, see section E, 'Types of sport children would do'. For what is meant by 'solitary', see appendix 2, which lists the questions which were used to score children as home-oriented or gregarious.

you think you are likely to be doing when you have finished full-time education?'

For children of high ability and high self-confidence, and for children of low ability and low self-confidence, the answers to both questions were often identical: to both questions the answer 'labourer' or 'machinist' or 'salesman' or 'banker' was given. The middle range had the knowledge and imagination to dream of a job pleasanter than one they were likely to get, and their answers were of the kind that had been expected: dream job—'air hostess', probable real job—'shop assistant'; dream job—'footballer', probable real job—'apprentice draughtsman'. The future machinist knew she would be a machinist and the notion of a 'dream job' was not very meaningful to her. The future banker had chosen the job he most wanted to do and was confident he would go on to do it. Thus similar replies giving identical 'dream' and 'realistic' future jobs reflected very different expectations of the future on the part of the children making them.

A similar unity of both extremes of ability occurred in the time taken to complete the questionnaire. Bright children took a long time because they saw possible ambiguities in wording; slow children took a long time partly because they too had difficulty in understanding the questions. The middle range responded quickly, had few doubts and on the whole interpreted questions as they had been intended. The closer a study gets to the people being studied, the less likely is it that such surface similarities will be misinterpreted as true similarities. Such difficulties to some extent can be avoided in an interview, and the follow-up questions were asked by interview in the home.

At this first stage of the enquiry the children were seen simultaneously, the leavers being gathered together in a few classrooms, and one or two members of the team supervised the administration in each room, answering questions and checking completed forms. Many doubts about definitions were discovered and cleared up in the classroom; the children were encouraged to ask questions, and every completed questionnaire was looked through. But it is not certain that equal care was taken in every classroom, in every school, and some of the problems were not exposed until visits to some schools had already been completed.

A second difficulty was that schools were visited on only one day in the year, when activities appropriate to the current season were fresh in the children's minds. Children were asked about activities participated in at other times of the year but children's memories and abilities to conceptualise and record clearly things they have done some months back vary considerably, so that these data are rather unreliable and have been treated as such. More reliance can be placed on precisely framed questions such as 'Between 5 and 6 p.m. yesterday what did you do?' but the answer 'Played football' to such a question gives no information about the importance sport has in the respondent's life.

One way of solving this difficulty is to ask the children directly about frequency—to say to them 'Do you play often, every now and then, or seldom?' or 'Do you play once a week in season, once a month, or less often than once a month in season?' Such a solution, however, relies on the memory or judgment of the child completing the questionnaire. In this research it was decided to give several opportunities, throughout the questionnaire, for the child to declare an interest in sport if he had it, and to count him as more actively interested in sport if he declared that interest in many responses than if he declared it in only a few. The index of sport-loving calculated for this purpose is described below.

A third difficulty is that to ask too many questions is to risk tiring the respondents, but to ask too few, restricted to too narrow a field, is to risk misinterpreting the meaning of the replies by isolating some activities and taking them from their context. To ask about sport and games only could perhaps lead the children to exaggerate the importance of sport and games in their lives and, further, could lead researchers, even without any exaggerations on the part of the children, to exaggerate the importance of physical activities in their lives. The words 'Playing football' in answer to the question 'Write down the three things you like doing best in the time after school' seem more useful than the same words would be, written in answer to the question 'What is your favourite sport?' Further, as will be seen from the above hypotheses, it was felt that more had to be known about the children than the sports they did, since what affected their interest in sports was relevant. Questions were asked, therefore, not only about physical recreation, but about general leisure interests and home background.

The questionnaire was divided into two sections and the first section given to the children was not concerned with sport. The questionnaire team was introduced as coming from the University and not from the Physical Education Department. Members of the team endeavoured to separate themselves from the staff of the school as far as was compatible with being courteous, and with keeping order among the children. It was hoped in this way to avoid the risk of bias which could have occurred if the team had been associated too closely in the children's minds with representatives of authority whose values the children would imagine they knew.

Several questions were asked which aimed in different ways at discovering the child's leisure activities. The answers to all these questions were then combined to give each child a score on an index of love of sport. A different group of questions was used to categorise each child as mainly interested in team games, in indoor sports and games or in outdoor recreation. .

Appendix 1 lists the questions[6] which were used to compile an index of sport-loving. These questions were chosen by the following technique. A sub-sample of 380 children's questionnaires was randomly chosen, and those children were given a crude 'love of sport' score on the basis of their answers to questions which on their face value indicated an interest or lack of interest in sport. The 100 children from the sub-sample scoring the highest, and the 100 scoring the lowest, crude love of sport scores were then taken, and each of their answers was tested with item discrimination tables to see which questions best discriminated between the high scorers and the low scorers. Questions which did not discriminate well were thrown out. The questions remaining became the basis for the index of sport-loving which was finally used for all the 2,685 children.

All the children in the sample were twice given stamped addressed cards on which to inform the University if they changed their addresses.

[6] E.g. 'Have you a hobby? TICK THE CORRECT ANSWER. Yes .... No .... If "Yes", name it: ....' If a sport was named as a hobby this was taken as scoring one 'sport-loving' point.

No claim is here made that the statements described above as hypotheses have been proved or disproved by the techniques used. Questions were asked of a substantial number of children from a well chosen sample of schools, and a preliminary analysis of their answers was made. This introduction describes some of the techniques used and makes clear some of the limitations of the research, and the results must be read with these techniques and limitations in mind. What is claimed is that the analysis throws some light on the factors which matter when considering provision for recreation; that it gives some clue as to which groups may need special attention, the most promising approaches, and the stages at which success is most likely to follow. A final report on the whole research will point to areas for possible future enquiry.

For the purposes of administering the questionnaire, a temporary research team was formed composed of members of the staff of the Physical Education Department and other helpers who had received a briefing. In this connection thanks are due to Mr Stephen Appleby, Miss Angela Bateman, Mrs Giovanna Bloor, Mrs Olive Chesworth, Mr Elwyn Griffiths, Mr Kevin Hardman, Miss Joyce Heron, Mr Andrew Macdonald, Mr David McNair, Mr David Morgan, Miss Joan Sheehan, Mr William Steel, Miss Betty Strutt, Mrs Irene Thomas and Mr Eric Ward.

Mr R. St. G. Harper, the Director, and the other members of the staff of the Physical Education Department helped unstintingly at each stage of the work, through discussion and in other ways; but neither they nor other helpers are responsible for the views expressed in this report. Miss Sheehan worked as a research assistant, though only paid as a secretary, and Mr Elwyn Griffiths was helpful throughout the research in very many ways. Professor Stephen Wiseman gave useful advice at an early stage, and conversations with Dr Cyril Smith, Director of Youth Studies at Manchester University, were useful at several stages of the research. Mr Tom Christie, lecturer in the Department of Education at Manchester University, and the late Mr Robin Emmett, of the statistical division of the South Wales Electricity Board, gave valued statistical advice and help. International Computing Services Ltd processed the data, and Miss B. E. Bibby of that company was an able and efficient helper. Mr Alan Hill kindly helped with the pie charts. The study was made possible by a generous grant from the Leverhulme Trust Fund and by the friendly co-operation of 2,685 young people and the Heads and teachers of their schools, to whom warmest thanks are due.

The author did not think it appropriate to use tests of significance and measures of correlation. Such statistics might have given a false appearance of precision to data many of which consist of crude indicators of the empirical relationships under discussion. Measures of correlation are used in section H for reasons explained therein.

I.E.

Results

The first point made clear by this enquiry is that sport and physical recreation play a subordinate part in the lives of many of the school leavers questioned.

Asked:

'What main sport, game or outdoor activity do you think you'll do AFTER you leave school or college? WRITE THE ANSWER. IF YOU ARE UNLIKELY TO DO ANY, WRITE "NONE" '

a third of the children in the sample wrote 'None'.

Given scores on an index of love of sport (see introduction and appendix 1), the highest scoring child scored 31 but over half the children scored less than 10.

Asked:

'If you could have any job you wanted when you left school or finished full-time education, what job would you choose?'

only 2.6 per cent of girls and 11 per cent of boys wrote as their dream job a job connected with sport.

Children in the sample were asked:

'Tick which one you would most like to be:

Boys	Girls
Businessman	Wife of a businessman
League footballer	Tennis champion
Pop singer	Pop singer
Scientist	Teacher
Doctor working in Africa	Nurse working in Africa'

In this question the notion of a glamorous sport career was directly suggested, but the majority of children still chose other things. Six per cent of the girls ticked 'tennis champion' and 30 per cent of the boys ticked 'league footballer'.

The results reported in the following pages should be read with this first finding in mind.

Section A. *Sex and sport*

The most marked, and perhaps the most obvious, result was the difference between boys and girls in their active interest in sport. The evidence from the data shows boys to be twice as sport-loving[1] as girls.

The mean sport-loving score for boys was 12; the mean sport-loving score for girls was 6. The median scores were 16 and 6. The modal, or most common, score for boys was 14 and for girls 3.

One question asked:

'What main sport, game or outdoor activity do you think you'll do AFTER you leave school or college? WRITE THE ANSWER. IF YOU ARE UNLIKELY TO DO ANY, WRITE "NONE".'

43·8 per cent of the girls wrote 'None' and 22·0 per cent of the boys wrote 'None'.

TABLE 1

Sport in relation to sex

Sport-loving score	Girls % n=1269	Boys % n=1416	Total % n
0-5 Non-sport-loving	75	25	100 = 833
6-11 Medium sport-loving	50	50	100 = 926
11+ Very sport-loving	19	81	100 = 926
Total	1269	1416	2685

Table 1 shows that in the category 'medium sport-loving' there were equal numbers of boys and girls: it is at the extremes that the difference shows. Three times as many girls as boys were non-sport-loving, and more than four times as many boys as girls were very sport-loving.

[1] The questions used in compiling sport-loving scores are listed in appendix 1.

17

Thus the evidence from this study supports the first hypothesis, that boys are more actively interested in sport than girls. Two considerations follow from this. First, it could be very misleading to look at data about sport-loving without first separating boys from girls, and so in most of the figures quoted below girls are separated from boys.

Second, those who make decisions in the field of recreational provision will have to use special approaches if they wish to attract the custom of girls in their teens to active recreation. Sections D and E below give some evidence of the particular sports, and the broad types of sport which appeal more to girls than to boys.

Section B. *Social class and sport*

The term 'social class' can refer to a person's class of origin—that is, to the way of life in which he was brought up—and it can also refer to the way of life he aspires to or has achieved or is achieving. For some school leavers in the sample the two will not correspond, and therefore in this discussion a distinction is made between class of origin and achievable class. In this report two indicators of social class are used. Each child was asked his father's occupation. The Registrar-General classifies occupations into five social classes, class 1 being described as professional, class 2 as intermediate, class 3 as skilled, class 4 as semi-skilled and class 5 as unskilled. Whilst there are many drawbacks to using this classification, it is the one which is the most comprehensive and therefore most widely used. To make the material in this study comparable with the material in other studies it was decided to use this classification. Father's occupation is a reasonable guide to class of origin.

The type of school attended is also a fair guide to class of origin and possibly a better guide to the future achieved class of young people. The majority of children from secondary modern schools, when they leave school, find work in classes 3, 4 and 5. Children from selective schools, whatever their class of origin, are more likely to find work in classes 1 and 2 than are children from secondary modern schools.

Table 2 shows the association between type of school attended and social class of origin as measured by the father's occupation. The Registrar-General puts 53 per cent of the population of Great Britain into class 3, "skilled occupations", and in the sample 54 per cent of the fathers' occupations fall into class 3. Here the comparison has been restricted to classes 1 and 2, which the Registrar-General calls 'professional' and 'intermediate' and which include occupations such as company director, manager, doctor, university lecturer, shop proprietor, teacher, farmer and electrical engineer.

The majority of Church secondary modern schools in this conurbation and all the Church secondary modern schools in

TABLE 2

Percentage of children in each type of school whose fathers' occupations fall into the Registrar-General's classes 1 and 2

	In Registrar-General's classes 1 and 2	Number representing 100%
Direct grant lay		
Girls	75.7	33
Boys	71.7	53
Direct grant Church		
Girls	40.0	50
Boys	58.8	34
Maintained grammar		
Girls	41.5	195
Boys	49.6	294
Maintained technical		
Girls	28.9	45
Boys	41.1	56
Secondary modern lay		
Girls	13.5	710
Boys	16.8	769
Secondary modern Church		
Girls	6.0	236
Boys	9.0	210

the sample are Catholic schools. The history of Irish immigration into the area and the tendency of Irish immigrants to find work mainly in unskilled occupations is associated with the fact that the Church schools have the most marked working class intake.

The division of direct grant schools into lay and Church reflects the fact that the ten Catholic direct grant schools (there is one Anglican direct grant school) in the conurbation take a greater proportion of children whose fees are paid by local authorities than do the twelve lay direct grant schools.[1] This is largely because there were no Catholic grammar schools functioning fully in the conurbation at the time of interview-

[1] For instance, Manchester Education Committee annually paid fees for children to take 160 places in four non-denominational direct grant schools in Manchester; and 295 places in five Roman Catholic direct grant schools, at the time of writing.

ing. The heads of Church direct grant schools said that their schools were far more comprehensive than the lay direct grant schools, and this the figures confirm, but direct grant Church schools for boys are still more middle class than maintained grammar schools.

The link between class and school attended is shown more simply when schools are divided into thirty selective (i.e. direct grant, maintained grammar and technical) and twenty-three unselective[2] (i.e. secondary modern) schools (see table 3).

TABLE 3

Percentage of children in sample in selective and unselective schools whose fathers' occupations fall into Registrar-General's classes 1 and 2 (relation between class of origin and type of school attended)

| | Selective schools (direct grant maintained technical and grammar) | | Unselective schools (secondary modern) | |
	Girls	Boys	Girls	Boys
R-G 1 and 2	43%	51.9%	11.6%	15.1%
	139	227	110	148
	100% = 323	100% = 437	100% = 946	100% = 979

The two indicators of social class—type of school attended and father's occupation—are thus related to each other. They are kept separate in this report, since school attended is taken to be an index of the class probably to be achieved in the future, whilst father's occupation is taken to be an index of social class of origin. More use will be made of this distinction in the follow-up than in this report.

TABLE 4(a)

The relationship between social class of origin and sport (omitting the Registrar-General's class 3): boys and girls together

	Registrar-General's classes 1 and 2	Registrar-General's classes 4 and 5
Non-sport-loving	23.6%	37.4%
Medium sport-loving	32.8%	37.0%
Very sport-loving	43.6%	25.6%
	100% = 624	100% = 430

[2] It should be remembered here that *all* the direct grant schools were visited but few leavers seen in each; whereas relatively few secondary modern schools were visited but many leavers seen in each.

C

Table 4(*a*) shows the children in the sample whose fathers' occupations fall into the Registrar-General's categories 1 and 2, which are here called middle class occupations, and whose fathers' occupations fall into the Registrar-General's categories 4 and 5, which are here called working class occupations, divided into the percentages in each sport-loving category.

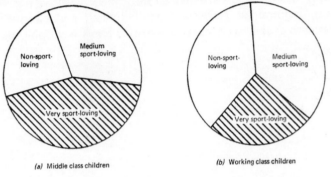

(a) Middle class children   *(b)* Working class children

FIG. 1

Fig. 1 shows the same data in pictorial form. This gives support to the second hypothesis, that middle class children are more sport-loving than working class children. The same data are shown separately for boys and girls in tables 4(*b*) and 4(*c*).

TABLE 4(*b*)

Proportions in working and middle classes who fall into three categories of sport-loving (omitting Registrar-General's class 3): girls

Registrar-General's classes	Non-sport-loving	Medium sport-loving	Very sport-loving	Total
1 and 2	38%	37%	25%	100% = 249
4 and 5	58%	34%	8%	100% = 223

TABLE 4(*c*)

Proportions in working and middle classes who fall into three categories of sport-loving (omitting Registrar-General's class 3): boys

Registrar-General's classes	Non-sport-loving	Medium sport-loving	Very sport-loving	Total
1 and 2	14%	30%	56%	100% = 375
4 and 5	16%	40%	44%	100% = 207

Tables 4(b) and 4(c) show those girls and boys whose fathers' occupations fall into the Registrar-General's categories 1 and 2, which are here called middle class occupations, and whose fathers' occupations fall into the Registrar-General's categories 4 and 5, which are here called working class occupations, divided into the proportions in each sport-loving category.

Fig. 2 shows the same data in pictorial form, and table 5 gives average sport-loving scores, shown separately for boys and girls. These data, too, show that among boys and far more markedly among girls there is a relationship between sport and class of origin as reflected in father's occupation—middle class children being clearly more sport-loving than working class children.

TABLE 5

Average sport-loving scores for each social class of origin

Father's occupation in Registrar-General's class	Median girls*	Mean girls	Median boys	Mean boys
1	10	10	13	12
2	7	7	13	12
3	6	6	12	12
4	5	6	11	12
5	5	5	9	10
Don't know	5	6	10	10

* Medians are shown as well as means in this kind of table where possible, since the distribution of sport-loving scores is not normal, and the intervals between each score are not known to be equal, and in these circumstances the median is a safer average to use than the mean.

There is thus evidence from this study to support the second hypothesis, that sport-loving youngsters are more commonly found among children of middle class origin than among children of working class origin, and this difference is much more marked for girls than for boys.

A similar result appears when one looks at the type of school attended, which is taken to be a fair guide to class of origin and a better guide to aspired class. Again, selective school girls, in particular, are more sport-loving than girls in secondary modern schools. (See table 6.)

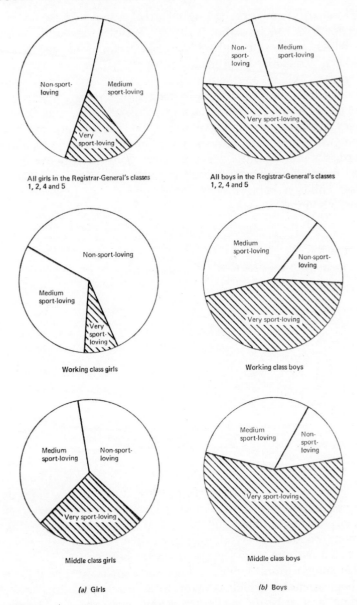

All girls in the Registrar-General's classes 1, 2, 4 and 5

All boys in the Registrar-General's classes 1, 2, 4 and 5

Working class girls

Working class boys

Middle class girls

Middle class boys

(a) Girls

(b) Boys

FIG. 2
Proportions in working and middle classes who fell into three categories of sport-loving, omitting the Registrar-General's class 3

TABLE 6

Average sport-loving scores for children attending different types of school*

	Girls		Boys	
	Median	Mean	Median	Mean
Selective .				
Direct grant lay	10	11	14	13
Direct grant Church	7	7	13	13
Maintained grammar	8	9	13	13
Maintained technical	7	8	10	11
All *selective* schools	8	9	13	13
Unselective				
Secondary modern Church	5	6	13	13
Secondary modern other	5	6	11	11
All *unselective* schools	5	6	11	12

* It should be noted that ten out of eleven Church direct grant schools in the conurbation are Catholic and that class of origin is more mixed in Catholic schools than in other direct grant schools because of the dearth of public provision of Catholic secondary schools (see section B above). There were only two technical schools in the sample (one in ten of twenty-two technical schools in the conurbation) and one of these was an art school. If it is correct to assume that children specialising in Art are less likely to be sport-loving than other children, other things being equal, then the figure for maintained technical schools may be biased.

Table 7 shows the percentages of girls and boys in each sport-loving category who attend selective and unselective schools.

TABLE 7

Respondents in selective and unselective schools in three categories of sport-loving

	Non-sport-loving (%)	Medium sport-loving (%)	Very sport-loving (%)	Total
(a) *Girls*				
Selective	31.5	41.0	27.5	100% = 323
Unselective	55.6	35.1	9.3	100% = 946
(b) *Boys*				
Selective	12.4	27.9	59.7	100% = 437
Unselective	15.0	35.0	50.0	100% = 979

There is thus evidence from this study to support the third hypothesis: that sport-loving youngsters are more commonly found in selective schools than in other schools, particularly in the case of girls.

Section C. *Age and sport*

The fourth hypothesis, that 14 and 15 year olds are more sport-loving than 16 and 17 year olds, is not borne out by the data. If the adult ethic, part of which is that sport is a 'good thing', weakens as the adolescent matures, and a stronger appeal of the adolescent sub-culture is felt, then one would expect this to show in a difference between age groups. However, the design of the present study does not make it easy to test this adequately, since children who stay at school after the legal school leaving age are probably not typical of their age group. They are preparing for examinations, and by definition almost, by the very act of staying on at school, show themselves to be more susceptible to adult values than their counterparts who leave school as soon as possible. An adequate test of the fourth hypothesis would have required the inclusion of 15 and 16 year olds who had left school, and the present study did not do this.

TABLE 8

Age in relation to sport: the whole sample, except for forty children aged 19

Age	Non-sport-loving (%)	Medium sport-loving (%)	Very sport-loving (%)	Total*
(a) Girls				
14	61.5	32.2	6.2	100% = 273
15	51.2	37.1	11.6	100% = 455
16	42.2	37.3	20.4	100% = 225
17	29.2	36.9	33.8	100% = 65
18	24.5	44.7	30.9	100% = 94
for all girls	49.5	36.6	13.9	100% = 1269
Age left blank	58.7	35.3	6.0	100% = 150
(b) Boys				
14	13.8	40.8	45.4	100% = 304
15	15.0	31.7	53.3	100% = 505
16	10.1	30.8	59.1	100% = 247
17	12.1	34.3	53.5	100% = 99
18	16.1	29.8	54.0	100% = 124
for all boys	14.5	32.6	52.9	100% = 1416
Age left blank	22.1	25.0	52.9	100% = 104

*When percentages do not total exactly 100% this is the approximation of the computer service..

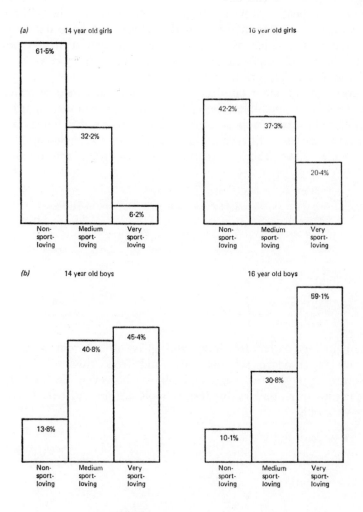

FIG. 3
Age in relation to love of sport

Table 8 shows the percentages of children in the sample of each age who fell into three categories of sport-loving, and from this it appears that active interest in sport increases as age increases in the case of girls, while in the case of boys there is a peak at the age of 16. Seven girls and thirty-three boys aged 19 were included in the sample but have not been shown in this table as they were so few that it would not have been meaningful to share them between categories. Some of the above data are represented in Fig. 3.

Most of the older children in the sample attended selective schools. It is possible, therefore, that in the above figures, differences which appear to be related to age differences are in fact related to differences in type of school attended and/or to social class. Table 9 therefore shows mean and median

TABLE 9

Average sport-loving scores for each age in children sampled in secondary modern schools only

(a) Girls			(b) Boys		
Age	Median	Mean	Age	Median	Mean
14	4	5	14	11	11
15	5	6	15	12	12
16	6	7	16	12	12
17	7	7	17	9	9

sport-loving scores for boys and girls of different ages in secondary modern schools only, and from them a similar picture emerges. As suggested above, however, 16 and 17 year olds in secondary modern schools are not typical 16 and 17 year olds.

Section D. *Participation in individual sports*

Several questions aimed at discovering the degree of participation in and popularity of particular sports, and these are numbered 1–4 in this section of the report only, to simplify comparison between them in the following discussion.

Question 1 asked:

'What games, sports, athletics or gymnastics do you take part in apart from those you take part in with or for the school? WRITE DOWN THEIR NAMES, AND HOW OFTEN YOU DO THEM, AND WHO WITH (i.e. with a team or club, or with a few friends). If none, write "None".'

Answers were coded under thirty-seven named sports, 'other' and 'none'. The answers most commonly given for boys and girls are shown in table 10.

TABLE 10

The percentage of boys and girls in the sample who said they played some sports outside school[*]

Girls	%[**]	Boys	%
None	56.7	Soccer	35.5
Tennis	12.5	None	30.0
Ten pin bowling	8.5	Table tennis	9.3
Netball	6.6	Tennis	8.6
Table tennis	6.2	Cricket	7.7
Ice skating	4.5	Other	7.6
Rounders	3.8	Ten pin bowling	6.0
Other	3.4	Cycling	5.7
Horse riding	2.8	Fishing	4.3
Badminton	2.3	Rugby	3.5
Roller skating	2.0	Golf	3.0
Cycling	1.4	Ice skating	2.7
Bowling on a green	1.2	Judo/karate	2.4
Hockey	1.2	Athletics	2.4
Athletics	1.1	Basketball	2.0
Gymnastics	1.1	Cross-country running	1.7
Golf	1.0	Badminton	1.6
Judo/karate	1.0	Bowling on a green	1.5
100% = 1269		100% = 1416	

[*] Swimming and rambling were asked about separately.
[**] These figures are true percentages.

Where the response of girls can be directly compared with the response of boys, more girls than boys said they played

29

tennis, ten pin bowling, ice skating, roller skating, horse riding, badminton (the percentage of boys doing horse riding being 0·4). In each case, arrangements can be made casually, the activities are often done in groups of mixed sexes, numbers are not fixed and dress usually can be individual and attractive.

Figures below show that very high proportions of girls said they went swimming and hiking or rambling, and similar comments could be made about these two sports.

Question 1(a) asked:

'Do you go swimming apart from when you go with or for the school? TICK THE CORRECT ANSWER. Yes .... No .... If "Yes", how often? ....'

Question 1(b) asked:

'Do you go hiking or rambling apart from when you go with or for the school? TICK THE CORRECT ANSWER. Yes .... No .... If "Yes" how often? ....'

The percentages of boys and girls who answered 'Yes' were as follows (the figures are true percentages):

	Girls	Boys
Swimming	55·4	66·7
Hiking or rambling	35·1	46·0

Question 2 asked:

'What games and sports do you play at school (apart from swimming, rambling, athletics and gymnastics)? WRITE DOWN THEIR NAMES, AND IF YOU LIKE ANY, UNDERLINE THEM.'

Answers to this question show which sports in school appeal to the non sport-loving and medium sport-loving and which sports in school are unpopular even with very sport-loving children.

It is easier *not* to underline a word one has written than it is to underline it, so it is not safe to assume that because a child did not underline a sport the child disliked that sport. But for the whole sample taken together, comparisons between sports on this basis are meaningful: if more people underlined one sport than they did another, provided a fair proportion did play those two sports at school, it is safe to say that the first sport is more popular when played at school than the second. Table 11 lists the seven sports for girls and the seven sports for boys which the highest proportion of children in the sample said they did at school.

TABLE 11

Sports most commonly done at school

	Girls in the sample who said they did it with the school %		Boys in the sample who said they did it with the school %
Netball	24.7	Soccer	24.2
Rounders	18.0	Cricket	14.6
Hockey	14.9	Basketball	13.4
Tennis	12.9	Rugby	11.5
Badminton	6.3	Cross-country	
Volleyball	4.2	running	7.9
Basketball	2.5	Tennis	5.1
		Badminton	4.4

For answers to question 2,[2] 100 per cent does not represent the number of girls or boys in the sport-loving category. 100 per cent represents the total number of times all coded activities were mentioned by children in each sport-loving category: i.e. number of activities mentioned multiplied by the number of times each was mentioned.

Table 12(a) shows the girls in the three sport-loving categories who said they did these sports at school and did or did not underline them.

Badminton was the only sport which was done at school by a substantial proportion of girls and which was 'liked' more often than 'disliked' by girls in each category of sport-loving. In the case of the other sports, more non-sport-loving girls 'disliked' than 'liked' the sport. Hockey and netball as played at school look particularly unpopular with this category of girls by comparison with other sports.[1]

Badminton, tennis and volleyball were the three sports which were done at school by a substantial proportion of girls and which were 'liked' more often than 'disliked' by medium sport-loving girls. More very sport-loving girls underlined the main sports they mentioned than did not underline them.

[1] Most questionnaires were administered between January and March 1966, when winter sports were being played at school, but see the results for cricket.

[2] Set out in tables 11, 12(a) and 12(b).

TABLE 12(*a*)

Sports commonly done at school and liked or disliked: girls

	Total	Non-sport-loving	Medium sport-loving	Very sport-loving
	%	%	%	%
Netball underlined, i.e. 'liked'	11.1	9.9	12.0	12.6
Netball not underlined.	13.6	16.2	12.9	8.5
Rounders underlined, i.e. 'liked'	8.7	8.6	8.5	9.1
Rounders not underlined	9.3	10.8	8.6	6.6
Hockey underlined, i.e. 'liked'	5.4	4.2	5.6	8.3
Hockey not underlined	9.5	10.6	9.6	6.4
Tennis underlined, i.e. 'liked'	7.6	5.2	8.6	11.3
Tennis not underlined	5.3	6.0	5.1	4.2
Badminton underlined, i.e. 'liked'	4.0	3.2	4.0	6.0
Badminton not underlined	2.3	1.8	2.9	2.3
Volleyball underlined, i.e. 'liked'	2.2	1.6	2.3	3.1
Volleyball not underlined	2.0	2.3	1.7	1.8
Basketball underlined, i.e. 'liked'	1.1	0.8	1.1	1.9
Basketball not underlined	1.4	1.7	1.3	0.6

TABLE 12(*b*)

Sports commonly done at school and liked or disliked: boys

	Total	Non sport-loving	Medium sport-loving	Very sport-loving
	%	%	%	%
Soccer underlined, i.e. 'liked'	13.3	7.0	13.0	14.7
Soccer not underlined	10.9	15.7	13.0	8.9
Cricket underlined i.e. 'liked'	6.1	3.5	5.1	7.1
Cricket not underlined	8.5	10.2	8.5	8.2
Basketball underlined, i.e. 'liked'	7.8	5.7	6.5	9.0
Basketball not underlined	5.6	6.0	5.5	5.6
Rugby underlined, i.e. 'liked'	5.8	3.2	5.7	6.4
Rugby not underlined	5.7	6.7	6.4	5.1
Cross-country running underlined, i.e. 'liked'	3.1	3.5	3.4	2.9
Cross-country running not underlined	4.8	6.2	5.1	4.3
Tennis underlined, i.e. 'liked'	3.7	2.2	3.7	3.9
Tennis not underlined	1.4	1.2	1.8	1.3
Badminton underlined, i.e. 'liked'	2.7	1.0	2.6	3.1
Badminton not underlined	1.7	1.7	1.5	1.8

Table 12(*b*) shows the boys in the three sport-loving categories who said they did seven sports at school and did or did not underline them.

Tennis is the one sport played by a substantial proportion of boys at school which is underlined, i.e. 'liked', by more non-sport-loving boys than disliked it.

Tennis, basket-ball and badminton are the three sports played by a substantial proportion of boys at school which were underlined, i.e. 'liked', by more medium sport-loving boys than disliked it.

Cross-country running and cricket are two sports which are unpopular as played at school, by this measure, among all categories of boys. More very sport-loving boys 'disliked' these two sports than 'liked' them.

Question 2(*a*) asked:

'Do you go swimming with the school? TICK THE CORRECT ANSWER.
Yes .... No .... If "Yes" do you like it?
Yes .... No ....'

The same question, in the same form, was asked about gymnastics, athletics and hiking/rambling. The answers cannot be directly compared to the answers to question 2, since these four sports were singled out. For none of the four sports did the majority who did them say they disliked them, as occurred in the earlier case with cricket and cross-country running. However, the summary of the replies, for boys and girls in all schools, in table 13(*a*) shows that athletics and gymnastics as

TABLE 13(*a*)

All children in all schools in the sample: popularity of hiking/rambling, gymnastics, swimming and athletics done with the school

	Hiking/ rambling		Gymnastics		Swimming		Athletics	
	Girls	Boys	Girls	Boys	Girls	Boys	Girls	Boys
	%	%	%	%	%	%	%	%
A Do and like	17.1	21.3	53.3	53.9	21.4	23.2	39.7	56.8
B Do and dislike	1.7	1.0	19.4	13.1	3.7	1.8	20.7	17.9
C Don't do	80.9	77.7	27.1	32.6	74.7	74.9	39.2	25.1
D Blank	0.3	—	0.2	0.4	0.2	0.1	0.4	0.3
100%	1269	1416	1269	1416	1269	1416	1269	1416

taught in school are less popular than swimming and hiking, and it also shows the high proportion of school leavers who said they did not go swimming or hiking/rambling with the school in their last year.

Of those who did each of these four activities with the school, the percentage who disliked them is shown in table 13(b).

TABLE 13(b)

Percentage of those doing all four activities who disliked them

	Hiking/ rambling		Gymnastics		Swimming		Athletics	
	Girls	Boys	Girls	Boys	Girls	Boys	Girls	Boys
B as percentage of A + B	9.2	4.4	26.7	19.4	14.7	7.1	34.3	23.9
100% =	239	316	923	949	319	354	766	1058

Question 3 asked:

'What main sport, game or outdoor activity do you think you will do AFTER you leave school or college? Write the answer. If you are unlikely to do any, write "NONE".'

The sports most frequently mentioned by girls and boys were as shown in table 14. The rest of the answers were distributed in very small proportions between other activities. Each child gave only one activity in answer to this question, and these are true percentages.

The most common answer for girls was 'None'. The activities which most girls favoured were tennis, swimming, netball, hiking, ten pin bowling and ice skating.

The most common answer for boys was 'soccer', and apart from the other main school sports, such as rugby, swimming and cricket, the outdoor pursuits—tennis, hiking, fishing, golf—and then some kind of self-defence were the activities most mentioned by boys.

The place of cycling is distorted here, as it was not coded separately but included in 'others'. 535 of the girls in the sample and 1,024 of the boys in the sample said they owned a bicycle.

Question 4 asked the children to tick sports which they had participated in during the twelve months preceding the filling in of the questionnaire, from a list containing 67 sports, games

TABLE 14

The choice of *one* sport for the future: some sports which children said they would do after leaving school

Girls	%	Boys	%
None	43.8	Soccer	29.0
Tennis	14.1	None	22.0
Swimming*	12.1	Rugby	4.9
Netball	5.0	Swimming	4.9
Hiking	4.1	Tennis	3.3
Ten pin bowling**	2.9	Cricket	3.0
Other***	2.7	Hiking	2.9
Ice skating	2.6	Other***	2.8
Badminton	1.7	Fishing	2.6
Hockey	1.5	Golf	2.5
Table tennis	1.3	Judo/karate/boxing/wrestling	2.2
Judo/karate/boxing/wrestling	1.2	Motor cycle racing	2.0
Keep fit/gymnastics	1.2	Athletics	1.8
Rounders	1.1	Shooting	1.8
Athletics	0.8	Table tennis	1.8
Roller skating	0.7	Basketball	1.1
Canoeing	0.4	Bowling on a green	1.1
Camping	0.3	Rock climbing	1.1
Ski-ing	0.3	Sailing	1.1
Basketball	0.2	Ten pin bowling	1.1
(100% = 1269)		(100% = 1416)	

* More girls than boys said they would, after leaving school, hike or swim. In section D above it will be seen that when asked whether they did hike and swim, more boys than girls said 'Yes'. It should be borne in mind that question 3, considered in this section, involved a choice: boys who put football had no chance to put swimming or hiking. When swimming and hiking were singled out, for a boy to say that he did swim or hike did not involve his saying 'No' about something else.

** There was a sudden growth in the provision of ten pin bowling alleys in the early 1960's and many failing cinemas were converted to this use. Ten pin bowling was still fashionable in the south-east Lancashire conurbation early in 1966, when most of the questionnaires were administered, but there is evidence that interest in the sport is not lasting. See *The Times*, 22 August 1967, and *The Observer*, 16 October 1966.

*** A miscellaneous category which, owing to coding error, included cycling.

and outdoor activities. The sports most often ticked in this question are shown in table 15. (Those sports ticked by fewer than 300 children have been omitted. The place of cycling may well have been distorted here by occurring on the list only as 'bicycle racing'.) In the answers to this question, activities done with the school are not separated from others.

At first sight, the answers to questions 1, 2, 3 and 4 might all be interpreted as indicating the popularity of individual sports. It will then be seen that these answers are not completely in agreement with each other. In particular, answers to question 2 could be read as showing cricket, cross-country running, hockey, netball and rounders to be unpopular; whilst answers to questions 1, 3 and 4 could show these same activities to be popular. Here the wording of each question must be borne in mind.

Question 4 asked what activities respondents had participated in during a twelve-month period, from a list of sports. The answers did not distinguish between sports done at or with the school on the one hand and sports done voluntarily, in free time, on the other. Thus the list in table 15 can be regarded only as evidence of participation in particular sports: the fact that a child has taken part in a sport does not mean that he or she enjoyed the participation. There is also some evidence that the

TABLE 15

Sports participated in during a twelve-month period

Swimming	1931	Rowing	706
Table tennis	1682	Rugby	653
Dancing*	1483	Bowling on a green	647
Tennis	1459	Boating	613
Gymnastics	1220	Organised rambling	567
Soccer	1111	Golf	556
Athletics	1089	Handball	484
Ten pin bowling	1076	Shooting outdoors	480
Netball	1059	Horse riding	468
Basketball	1014	Canoeing	461
Cross-country running	1007	Judo/karate	428
Badminton	995	Rock climbing	417
Cricket	962	Keep fit	385
Volleyball	936	Sailing	367
Ice skating	813	Shooting indoors	344
Hockey	774	Pleasure craft cruising	338
Roller skating	735	Archery	309
Fishing	724	Baseball	308

* Dancing here was dancing apart from ballet, ballroom or folk dancing, and mainly means dancing to modern popular music.

words 'in the last twelve months' were not always noticed or taken seriously. A list of sports was put in front of the children at the latter end of the questioning. Until that time, hardly any sports had been named for them. Their memories refreshed, they recalled sports they had tried, and there was a temptation for those who had participated in an activity once, longer ago than twelve months, to tick that activity.

Question 3 asked what game or sport respondents thought they would do when they left school. Answers to this question are clearly related to popularity: children were here asked to choose one sport. However, they were asked to predict, by an act of imagination, what they would do in the future, and, because of this, answers to this question cannot be regarded as so reliable as those which result from a child's recollection of events in his recent past.

Question 2 asked what sports were done in and with the school, and, of these, which were liked and which were disliked. This question asked directly about popularity and asked for a recollection of events in the respondent's recent past but referred only to sports done in and with the school. When table 12(b) shows that a majority of those boys who did cricket and cross-country running at school 'did not like' those sports, the table is not showing that most boys do not like cricket and cross-country running, but that most boys in the sample who did cricket and cross-country running at school did not like doing these things at school. The implication is that there is something about the way these sports are organised and played at school which is unpopular, and other tables show that, outside school, cricket is one of the most popular boys' sports, although the same is not true of cross-country running.

Question 1 asked children to name sporting activities done outside school. It is safe to assume that children know what games and sports they do in their spare time and that they do them largely because they like them. They are limited in what they do by lack of facilities, lack of knowledge and training and by the fact that seldom, at school or elsewhere, have they been introduced to a wide range of physical activities. The sports they commonly play at school influence the sports they commonly play in their spare time. Nevertheless, if they take the trouble to play sport A rather than sport B in their spare time, this can be read as evidence that they like to play sport A; though it cannot be read as evidence that they do not like sport B or would not like it if they could more easily play it.

Thus answers to question 1 in this section are the most reliable pointer to the popularity of and voluntary participation in individual sports; answers to question 2 give reliable evidence on the popularity of individual sports as played at school; answers to question 3 give less reliable evidence on the popularity of particular sports; and answers to question 4 give evidence only on participation in particular sports, slightly distorted by variance in memory and in the degree to which the time limitation was adhered to. Answers to all four questions

D

have been reported on partly because each question probed into one interesting aspect of the subject, and partly to expose some of the snags met in interpreting responses to such questions.

Taking questions 1, 3 and 4 only, and ignoring for the moment question 2, which relates to sports done only in school, the placing of table tennis is worth noting. Table tennis was chosen by relatively few children as the sport or game they thought they would do after leaving school: but it came high on the list of sports actually participated in, as shown by responses to question 1 and particularly to question 4. This discrepancy may be connected with the availability of table tennis tables in youth clubs and other institutions and the ease with which the game is played all the year round. It is possible that table tennis is not a game that people hope or plan to do so much as a game that they do in fact do, at this age.

Section E.   *Types of sport children would do*

Physical activities were divided into three groups as follows:

Indoor sports and games	Team games	Outdoor recreation
Table tennis	Soccer	Swimming
Ten pin bowling	Cricket	Tennis
Roller skating	Rugby	Golf
Ice skating	Netball	Fishing
Squash	Hockey	Rambling
Badminton	Rounders	Croquet
Fencing	Lacrosse	Sailing
Boxing	Volleyball	Rowing
Wrestling	Basketball	Boating
Judo	Handball	Rock climbing
Weight-lifting	Baseball	Pot holing
Gymnastics	Four/five-a-side	Horse riding
Fives	football	Bowling on a green
Keep fit	Athletics	Shooting outdoors
Dance	Cross-country	Archery
Indoor shooting	running	Surfing
		Water ski-ing
		Aqualung diving
		Canoeing
		Pleasure craft cruising
		Caving
		Ski-ing
		Pony trekking
		Gliding

The classification was not made with the intention of its use for any other purposes than those of the present study. It was made with reference to a population composed of school leavers in a conurbation, not one composed of active enthusiasts and specialists in sport. Where there is any doubt as to the meaning of a word, the meaning here taken is that which would be most commonly understood or intended by a moderately well informed 15 year old school leaver in an urban secondary modern school. Thus rowing and swimming may be highly competitive team sports for many enthusiasts in these sports, but for the majority of teenagers who participate in the activities which they mean to describe when they use these words, rowing and swimming are forms of unstructured recreation.

The classification here made is not based primarily on the presence or absence of competitiveness, type of skill required, or type of land use or geographical location involved, though these factors were employed in the classification. The main underlying criterion was social. An attempt was made to distinguish between broad groups of physical activities which involve social interaction of a like kind.

Thus under the heading 'Team games' the main aim was to group those sports which call for fixed numbers of performers playing particular roles in a team which is pitted against another similar team. To continue these sports after school it is usually necessary to join a club and to have reached a certain degree of ability. Games have to be organised; appointments to meet other teams made.

Under the heading 'Indoor sports and games' the main aim was to group those activities which are usually conducted indoors, can usually be combined easily with social functions and can be engaged in casually without much prior arrangement and without too great a dependence on fixed numbers of participants.

Under the heading 'Outdoor recreation' an attempt was made to group activities which usually take place in the open country and in which desires for space, fresh air and unstructured physical recreation are some of the main motives. These activities carry an overt sociable role, and can be engaged in casually without much prior arrangement and without too great a dependence on fixed numbers of participants.

An attempt was made to put each activity considered into one or other of the three categories, and the final decision sometimes rested on a particular activity being more akin to one group than another, rather than on that particular activity fitting a definition implied in the title of the group.

There is a considerable degree of overlapping between such definitions. It may be advisable to join a club in order to become an angler of a certain standard. Teams of swimmers may be formed to enter into competitive events. It would not be appropriate to describe wrestling or judo as engaged in casually. Swimming is far more often done indoors than outdoors. Furthermore, for the purposes of inferring trends, it might have been better to have treated swimming and tennis as a separate category, since they have long been the most popular sports among girls, and their inclusion among outdoor recreation swells the numbers predominantly interested in that category in a misleading fashion when outdoor recreation is being seen as a fast-growing category. However, in the total study, this will not be important; in the follow-up, swimming and tennis will again be included in outdoor recreation and trends will be far more visible. And whilst some swimming is done by teams and most swimming is done indoors, most swimming participated in by teenagers is engaged in casually, has as its main motive unstructured physical exercise, and takes place in a building which does not provide for sociable interaction in the same way as a bowling alley, skating rink or youth club does.

Whilst wrestling and judo can hardly be engaged in casually, most self-defence which is participated in by teenagers takes place in youth clubs. Similarly the predominant motive in fishing is a desire for fresh air, space and unstructured physical exercise. A case can be made out for the allocation of most sports categorised as indoor, outdoor or team in the way detailed above, if the underlying criterion of type of social interaction is borne in mind, and if it is also borne in mind that non-specialist definitions are used.

Children were asked:

'Are there any other sports, games or outdoor activities (other than the sports you play in school) which you don't play regularly but which you have thought of taking up regularly if you had the chance? TICK THE CORRECT ANSWER. Yes .... No .... If "Yes", write down their names and the reasons why you don't play them.'

The analysis of answers to this question by individual sports is given in Appendix 5.

The individual sports given in answer to this question were coded as indoor games, outdoor recreation or team games on the basis described above, and the results are shown in table 16.

TABLE 16

Type of sports other than school sports which respondents would like to do outside school but don't do, in relation to sport-loving categories

	Non-sport-loving (%)	Medium sport-loving (%)	Very sport-loving (%)	Total (%)
(a) *Girls*				
Indoor	7.2 Fa	12.5 Fa	21.5 Fa	11.2
Outdoor	8.8 Fa	13.0 Fa	22.6 Fa	12.3
Team	2.9 Tr	3.7 Fa	5.7 Fa/Tr	3.5
None	81.2	70.6	50.3	73.0
Blank	—	—	—	—
	100% = 628	100% = 464	100% = 177	
(b) *Boys*				
Indoor	6.0 Fa	11.0 Fa	13.8 Fa	11.8
Outdoor	16.2 Fa	16.7 Ex	18.4 Ex	17.4
Team	2.5 Tr	5.0 Fa	7.2 Fa	5.8
None	75.5	67.3	60.2	64.7
Blank	—	—	0.3	0.1
	100% = 205	100% = 462	100% = 749	

The answer most commonly given to this question was 'None', but the type of sport most often mentioned by those who answered 'Yes' was outdoor recreation, with indoor sports and games coming second and team games last.[1]

The letters by the side of each figure in tables 16(a) and (b) indicate the reason most commonly given by that group as to why the sport was not pursued. Reasons were coded as:

> Fr Friends will not
> Fa Facilities far or lacking
> Ex Expense
> Tr Training and help lacking or respondent not
> good enough at the sport.

In the lettering of tables 16(a) and (b) 'other reasons' were ignored. Joint coding such as Fa/Fr means that as many gave

---

[1] Another question, the answers to which are not tabulated here, asked what school sports respondents would like to do outside school but don't do, and the affirmative answers to this question most often mentioned team sports.

'friends will not' as a reason as gave 'facilities lacking or far' as a reason. A consideration of the reasons children gave as to why they had not done the sports they would have liked to showed that lack of facilities or distance from facilities was the reason most commonly given, lack of training was of some significance for team sports, and two groups of boys gave expense as the reason why they did not pursue the outdoor recreation they would have liked to pursue. A lack of facilities for all kinds of physical recreation, the lack of adequate training in the case of team sports, and the expense of some kinds of out-door recreation will be part of the explanation of why a favour-able attitude is often not translated into active participation.

Section F. *Individual sports and social class*

The question[1] was asked:

'What games, sports, athletics or gymnastics do you take part in apart from those you take part in with or for the school? WRITE DOWN THEIR NAMES, AND HOW OFTEN YOU DO THEM, AND WHO WITH [i.e. with a team or club or with a few friends]. If none, write "None".'

Answers were analysed by social class of origin as indicated by the place of father's occupation in the Registrar-General's classification. The results are as shown in tables 17(*a*) and (*b*) for the answers most commonly given.

For girls, tennis, ten pin bowling, ice skating, rounders, table tennis, horse riding, badminton and athletics are middle class sports, whilst netball, gymnastics, bowling on a green and hockey show as working class sports by this measure.

For boys, tennis, golf, ice skating, ten pin bowling, fishing, table tennis and cricket are middle class sports by this measure, whilst soccer, rugby and athletics show as working class sports by this measure.

For both sexes, the 'None' responses confirm that working class children are less interested in active sport than are middle class children and that this relationship is more marked in the case of girls than in the case of boys.

The figures here are not percentages of all girls and boys in each class, but percentages of the total number of activities mentioned multiplied by the number of times they were mentioned.

Swimming and hiking were asked about separately. Table 18(*a*) shows the responses to the question 'Do you go swimming apart from when you go with or for the school?' Table 18(*b*) shows the responses to the question 'Do you go hiking or rambling apart from when you go with or for the school?' By this

[1] This question is the question 1 discussed near the end of section D and described there as a reliable guide to popularity, and here used in a different context.

TABLE 17(a)

Some sports done out of school by girls in relation to social class of origin, excluding class 3

	Registrar-General's classes 1 and 2	Registrar-General's classes 4 and 5
	%	%
None	29.3	59.0
Tennis	16.6	5.9
Ten pin bowling	11.6	2.3
Netball	3.0	8.3
Table tennis	6.1	3.5
Ice skating	5.0	2.4
Rounders	4.3	1.9
Horse riding	3.6	1.2
Badminton	2.8	0.8
Roller skating	1.7	1.6
Cycling	1.1	0.8
Bowling on a green	0.8	1.2
Athletics	1.4	—
Hockey	0.8	1.1
Judo/karate	0.8	0.4
Gymnastics	—	1.2
	100% = 362	100% = 254

TABLE 17(b)

Some sports done out of school by boys in relation to social class of origin, excluding class 3

	Registrar-General's classes 1 and 2	Registrar-General's classes 4 and 5
	%	%
Soccer	18.6	29.0
None	14.1	24.8
Table tennis	7.0	5.3
Tennis	9.3	2.1
Cricket	6.1	4.6
Ten pin bowling	5.3	3.5
Cycling	3.6	2.5
Fishing	3.5	1.4
Rugby	1.8	4.2
Golf	4.3	0.7
Ice skating	3.7	0.7
Judo/karate	2.0	2.1
Athletics	1.0	2.5
Basketball	0.5	1.1
Bowling on a green	1.4	1.1
	100% = 625	100% = 283

measure, hiking ranks with the middle class sports, for both sexes.

TABLE 18(a)

Percentage of boys and girls in the Registrar-General's classes 1 and 2, and the Registrar-General's classes 4 and 5, who said they did go swimming apart from when they went with or for the school

	Registrar-General's classes 1 and 2	Registrar-General's classes 4 and 5
Girls	59	50
Boys	68	60

TABLE 18(b)

Percentage of boys and girls in the Registrar-General's classes 1 and 2, and in the Registrar-General's classes 4 and 5, who said they did go hiking or rambling apart from when they went with or for the school

	Registrar-General's classes 1 and 2	Registrar-General's classes 4 and 5
Girls	52	23
Boys	52	35

Individual sports in selective and unselective schools

The figures in tables 19(a) and (b) show the percentages of each sex in selective and unselective schools who said they did various sports outside school (in answer to question 1 discussed in section D).

In table 19(a) sports participated in by ten or fewer girls have been omitted. Percentages here are percentages of girls attending each type of school who said they did the sport. Some girls mentioned several sports, so that if the columns were added up the totals would be more than 100 per cent. In table 19(b) sports participated in by fewer than twenty boys have been omitted.

Table 20 shows the percentages of each sex in selective and unselective schools who said they would do various sports after they left school. One sport was given by each child.

TABLE 19(a)

Percentage of girls in selective and unselective schools who said they did some sports out of school*

	Selective	Unselective
None	27.9	66.5
Tennis	31.3	6.1
Ten pin bowling	24.8	2.9
Netball	5.3	7.1
Table tennis	11.1	4.5
Ice skating	10.2	2.5
Rounders	5.9	3.1
Horse riding	6.2	1.6
Badminton	4.9	1.4
Roller skating	4.0	1.3
Cycling	1.9	1.2
Bowling on a green	1.2	1.3
Athletics	2.5	0.7
Hockey	1.2	1.2
Gymnastics	-	1.5
Judo/karate	1.2	0.9
Golf	1.8	0.6
Other	5.9	2.5
	100% = 323	100% = 946

* Swimming and rambling were asked about separately.

TABLE 19(b)

Percentage of boys in selective and unselective schools who said they did some sports out of school*

	Selective	Unselective
Soccer	31.5	37.1
None	20.8	34.1
Table tennis	14.0	7.1
Tennis	20.9	3.1
Cricket	9.4	6.9
Ten pin bowling	12.8	3.0
Cycling	6.9	5.2
Fishing	5.5	3.8
Rugby	3.4	3.5
Golf	6.6	1.4
Ice skating	5.5	1.4
Judo/karate	3.4	1.9
Athletics	1.8	2.6
Basketball	1.6	2.1
Badminton	2.5	1.1
Cross-country running	1.4	1.7
Bowling on a green	2.6	1.0
Camping	0.7	1.6
Sailing	3.6	0.2
Canoeing, rowing, boating	2.0	0.9
Other	7.6	7.6
	100% = 437	979

* Swimming and rambling were asked about separately.

TABLE 20

Percentage of girls and boys in selective and unselective schools who would do one particular sport after leaving school

	Total number of children who gave each answer	Girls		Boys	
		Selective	Un-Selective	Selective	Un-selective
None	868	20.4	51.8	12.8	26.1
Soccer	410	—	—	21.3	32.4
Tennis	226	32.2	7.9	7.6	1.4
Swimming	222	12.1	12.1	5.0	4.8
Hiking	93	8.0	2.7	3.7	2.6
Other*	74	1.5	3.1	4.1	2.2
Rugby	70	—	—	8.7	3.3
Netball	63	3.1	5.6	—	—
Ten pin bowling	53	2.8	3.0	1.6	0.9
Judo/karate boxing/wrestling	46	1.9	1.0	2.3	2.1
Ice skating	43	1.9	2.9	1.4	0.4
Cricket	42	—	—	4.6	2.2
Table tennis	42	1.5	1.3	1.8	1.7
Fishing	39	—	0.2	3.0	2.5
Golf	37	—	0.1	4.3	1.7
Athletics	36	1.2	0.6	2.7	1.4
Badminton	34	4.3	0.8	1.4	0.6
Motor cycle racing	31	—	0.2	1.4	2.3
Shooting	25	—	—	0.9	2.1
Camping	19	0.6	0.2	0.5	1.3
Hockey	19	3.1	1.0	—	—
Sailing	19	0.9	—	2.5	0.5
Basketball	18	—	0.2	1.4	1.0
Rock climbing	18	0.3	0.2	2.1	0.6
Keep fit/Gymnastics	17	—	1.6	—	0.2
Car rallying	14	0.3	0.1	1.1	0.7
Rounders	14	0.9	1.2	—	—
Weight-lifting	13	—	—	0.2	1.2
Lacrosse	11	0.3	—	1.4	0.4
Canoeing	10	—	0.5	0.2	0.4
Roller skating	10	1.2	0.5	—	0.1
Pot-holing	6	0.3	—	0.5	0.3
Fencing	6	0.6	0.1	0.2	0.1
Ski-ing	5	0.3	0.3	0.2	—
Surfing	5	—	0.2	0.2	0.2
Flying	4	—	—	—	0.4
Bowling on a green	3	—	—	0.2	0.2
Squash	2	—	—	0.2	0.1
Rowing	2	—	0.1	—	0.1
Volleyball	2	—	—	0.2	0.1
This question left blank	15	—	0.5	0.2	0.9
100% =		323	946	437	979

* 'Other' included cycling and horse riding.

Section G. *Types of sport and social class*

There is some evidence that both in Britain and abroad[1] working class people emulate middle class leisure activities and, after a time lag, catch up. Thus, for example, golf, ski-ing, sailing, rock climbing and mountaineering have spread their appeal down the social scale in the post-war years. The money, time and curiosity needed to try new things are all more commonly found among middle class than among working class people.

One of the main changes taking place in sport at present is thought to be a growth in the popularity of outdoor recreation of a relatively unorganised kind. Part of this growth can probably be accounted for by the catching up process referred to above.

If it were the case that current growth in outdoor pursuits was partly explicable in terms of the catching up process, then figures for the relative popularity of different kinds of sport might not distinguish markedly between classes at this age level. However, unevenness in the development could be expected. It was therefore thought worthwhile to look at the data from the south-east Lancashire school leavers with this change in mind, and the fifth hypothesis was included: that 'as opposed to team games, outdoor recreation is more commonly taken up by middle class than working class children, and by selective school children than other children'.

Children in the sample were categorised as mainly interested in team games, indoor sports and outdoor recreation on the basis of their answers to the questions listed in appendix 4. Maximum possible scores for each type of sport varied, and the scores were made comparable by conversion with Pearson's table 1.[2] It was possible for a child to have an equal score for

[1] Madame Nicole Samuel addressed a conference on leisure organised by the British Sociological Association in 1967 and reported that those working in the field of leisure in France based future plans partly on an assumption that what middle class people did with their leisure today would be done by working class people with their leisure in the future.

[2] Table of deviates of the normal curve for each per mille of frequency.

any two or all three of the types of sport, but in fact the only combination which occurred was indoor/outdoor: a few scored as many indoor as outdoor points and are categorised as equally interested in both. The way in which sports were divided is described in section E above.

TABLE 21(a)

Type of sport in relation to sex

	Team games		Indoor sports and games		Outdoor recreation		Equal indoor/ outdoor		Total
	n	%	n	%	n	%	n	%	
Girls	267	21.0	393	31.0	592	46.7	17	1.3	100% = 1269
Boys	637	45.0	491	34.7	285	20.1	3	0.2	100% = 1416
	904		884		877		20		2685

TABLE 21(b)

Type of sport in relation to sex, for three categories of sport loving: all the children in the sample

	Team (%)	Indoor (%)	Outdoor (%)	Equal indoor/outdoor (%)	
	Non-sport-loving children				
Girls	28.5	27.7	42.2	1.6	100% = 628
Boys	44.9	33.7	21.0	0.5	100% = 205
	Medium sport-loving children				
Girls	12.9	35.1	50.4	1.5	100% = 464
Boys	33.3	46.1	20.6	—	100% = 642
	Very sport-loving children				
Girls	15.8	31.6	52.5	—	100% = 177
Boys	52.2	27.9	19.6	0.3	100% = 749

Table 21(a) shows the numbers and percentages of girls and boys, from all schools and all classes, who were scored as being predominantly interested in team, indoor or outdoor recreation or equally in indoor and outdoor.

These data show more than twice as many girls to be interested predominantly in outdoor recreation as there were girls predominantly interested in team games, and more than twice as many boys to be interested predominantly in team games as there were predominantly interested in outdoor recreation.

When these results are broken down into sport-loving categories the largest group among each category of girls is that of girls interested predominantly in outdoor recreation. In the case of boys, the largest group of medium sport-loving boys are interested predominantly in indoor sports and games whilst for non-sport-loving and very sport-loving boys, team games are the most popular type of sport. See table 21(b).

Table 22 shows the percentages of girls and boys whose fathers' occupations are in the Registrar-General's classes 1 and 2, which are here called middle class, on the one hand, and in the Registrar-General's classes 4 and 5, which are here called working class, on the other hand, who favoured each different type of sport.

TABLE 22

Type of sport in relation to social class of origin, excluding class 3

Registrar-General's classes	Team games	Indoor sports and games	Outdoor recreation	Equal indoor/ outdoor	Total
(a) Girls %	%	%	%	%	
1 and 2	17.7	38.5	43.4	0.4	100% = 249
4 and 5	25.6	29.6	43.5	1.3	100% = 223
(b) Boys					
1 and 2	35.5	41.6	22.9	0.0	100% = 375
4 and 5	54.6	28.0	17.4	0.0	100% = 207

The most marked difference shown in this table is the class difference in preference for indoor sports and games. Whereas most working class boys were categorised as preferring team games, the largest group of middle class boys were those categorised as preferring indoor games and in the case of girls there is a similar, though not so large difference.

The fifth hypothesis receives no confirmation from this table in the case of girls, and some support in the case of boys: middle class boys were more often interested in outdoor recreation than were working class boys.

The figures are broken down between sport-loving categories in tables 23(a) and (b). These tables show that in the case of very and non-sport-loving girls and medium and very sport-loving boys, greater proportions of middle class than of working class children preferred outdoor recreation. Among medium sport-loving girls the class difference shows in indoor sports and games, and in table 22 this group hid the middle class preference for outdoor recreation in the other two groups. Among non-sport-loving boys a greater proportion of working class than of middle class boys preferred outdoor recreation and a greater proportion of middle class than of working class

TABLE 23(a)

Type of sport in relation to social class of origin excluding class 3, in three sport-loving categories: girls

Registrar-General's classes	Team games (%)	Indoor sports and games (%)	Outdoor recreation (%)	Equal indoor/ outdoor (%)	Total
		Non-sport-loving			
1 and 2	25.5	30.8	42.6	1.1	100% = 94
4 and 5	30.2	29.5	38.8	1.5	100% = 129
		Medium sport-loving			
1 and 2	14.0	42.0	44.0	—	100% = 93
4 and 5	15.8	27.6	55.3	1.3	100% = 76
		Very sport-loving			
1 and 2	11.3	45.2	43.5	—	100% = 62
4 and 5	33.3	38.9	27.8	—	100% = 18

TABLE 23(b)

Type of sport in relation to social class of origin excluding class 3, in three sport-loving categories: boys

Registrar-General's classes	Team games (%)	Indoor sports and games (%)	Outdoor recreation (%)	Equal indoor/ outdoor (%)	Total
		Non-sport-loving			
1 and 2	45.3	39.6	15.1	—	100% = 53
4 and 5	46.9	25.0	28.1	—	100% = 32
		Medium sport-loving			
1 and 2	21.4	54.5	24.1	—	100% = 112
4 and 5	44.6	39.7	15.7	—	100% = 83
		Very sport-loving			
1 and 2	40.5	35.2	24.3	—	100% = 210
4 and 5	66.3	18.5	15.2	—	100% = 92

boys preferred indoor games, and in table 22 this group hid the extent to which a greater proportion of middle class than working class boys preferred outdoor recreation in the other two groups.

To summarise the evidence bearing on the fifth hypothesis: it is true for those children who are actively interested in sport that more children of middle class than of working class origin are predominantly interested in outdoor recreation. There is a more marked class difference in the case of indoor sports.

TABLE 24

Percentage of children in sample in selective and unselective schools who were predominantly interested in team, indoor or outdoor sports

	Team	Indoor	Outdoor	Equal indoor/ outdoor	Total
(a) Girls					
Selective	17.0	30.7	52.0	0.3	100% = 323
Unselective	22.4	31.1	44.8	1.7	100% = 946
					1269
(b) Boys					
Selective	41.2	35.2	23.6	0.0	100% = 437
Unselective	46.7	34.4	19.6	0.3	100% = 979
					1416

Table 24 shows type of sport in secondary modern and in other schools, for boys and girls. These figures give some support to the fifth hypothesis. Though most boys in both kinds of school favoured team games, and most girls in both kinds of school favoured outdoor recreation, girls and boys in selective schools expressed a preference for outdoor recreation more often than did girls and boys in secondary modern schools.

The figures are broken down between sport-loving categories in tables 25(a) and (b). Here, as in table 23(b), it can be seen that a high proportion of medium sport-loving boys of both classes are predominantly interested in indoor sports and games, but for boys a breakdown by type of school attended shows a similar picture to that shown by the breakdown by class of origin: among boys very interested in sport a greater proportion from selective schools than from unselective schools are

E

predominantly interested in outdoor sport. Again, the class difference is greater for indoor sport, in this group.

TABLE 25(a)

Type of sport in relation to type of school attended, in three sport-loving categories: girls

	Team games (%)	Indoor sports and games (%)	Outdoor recreation (%)	Equal indoor/ outdoor (%)	Total
	Non-sport-loving				
Selective	27.5	23.5	48.0	1.0	100% = 102
Unselective	28.7	28.5	41.1	1.7	100% = 526
	Medium sport-loving				
Selective	12.1	32.6	55.3	—	100% = 132
Unselective	13.3	36.1	48.5	2.1	100% = 332
	Very sport-loving				
Selective	12.3	36.0	51.7	—	100% = 89
Unselective	19.3	27.3	53.4	—	100% = 88

TABLE 25(b)

Type of sport in relation to type of school attended in three sport-loving categories: boys

	Team games (%)	Indoor sports and games (%)	Outdoor recreation (%)	Equal indoor/ outdoor (%)	Total
	Non-sport-loving				
Selective	42.6	37.0	20.4	—	100% = 54
Unselective	45.7	32.4	21.2	0.7	100% = 151
	Medium sport-loving				
Selective	31.1	41.8	27.1	—	100% = 122
Unselective	34.1	47.7	18.2	—	100% = 340
	Very sport-loving				
Selective	45.6	31.8	22.6	—	100% = 261
Unselective	55.7	25.8	18.0	0.4	100% = 488

In the case of girls the picture is not the same. There are greater proportions of girls from selective than from unselective schools predominantly interested in outdoor recreation only among the non- and medium sport-loving categories. In the very sport-loving group the selective school bias occurs in the case of indoor sports and games.

Section H. *School provision and sport*

Schools vary in their facilities for games, gymnastics and sports: some have their own swimming pool, some have new, well-equipped gymnasia, some have enthusiastic PE staff, some are situated near the country and are able to take advantage of this; others have virtually no facilities.

There is a shortage of PE teachers in the conurbation, and schools in the decaying parts of the city and town centres often have difficulty in attracting PE teachers.

In judging the effect of school provision on young people's lasting interest in physical recreation, one needs to rank schools according to the standard of provision they offer. The ranking has been made only for secondary modern schools, since the influence of differential finance available and the influence of social origin of pupils and teachers are diminished by confining the comparison to one between secondary modern schools. However, a further variable intrudes when ranking schools, and that is the actual number of children seen in each school; this number should be borne in mind, particularly in this section.

The following questions[1] were taken to be relevant to such a ranking:

'Do you do gymnastics at school? TICK THE CORRECT ANSWER. Yes .... No ....'

'Do you do athletics at school? TICK THE CORRECT ANSWER. Yes .... No ....'

'Do you go hiking or rambling with the school? TICK THE CORRECT ANSWER. Yes .... No ....'

'Do you go swimming with the school? TICK THE CORRECT ANSWER. Yes .... No ....'

[1] Each of the first four questions was followed by the subsidiary question: 'If "Yes", do you like it?' After the fifth question the instruction appeared: 'Write down their names and, if you like any, underline them'. In the following discussion only the answers 'No' are used, but the fact that children had an opportunity to say that they did something but didn't like it probably reduced the number who said 'No' when they meant 'Yes, but as seldom as possible because I dislike it.'

'What games and sports do you play at school (apart from the activities already mentioned on this page)?'

Schools were ranked according to the mean percentage of children of each sex in each school who said they did not swim, ramble, do gymnastics or do athletics with the school; and were separately ranked by the range of sports mentioned by all children of each sex in answer to the question 'What games and sports do you play at school (apart from the activities already mentioned on this page)?' The second ranking was probably more influenced by the numbers seen in each school than was the first ranking.

It should also be noted with reference to the second ranking that whilst the offering of a wide range of sports usually indicates an active effort to interest the non-sport-loving in physical recreation, such an offer is frequently open to a minority of the school population.

Perhaps it needs to be mentioned here that ranking schools in these ways implies no reflection on the schools which rank low, for a variety of reasons. Some schools, such as AG, FG, HB, KG, GB, and DB, are situated in old buildings in slums; without playing fields, distant from parks, with prefabricated classrooms spreading over the playground; with conditions generally which make it extremely hard to attract adequate staff; and in districts such that it is very common for staff to live very far from the school. In such circumstances, schools Heads—often, in the author's experience, among the most hopeful, energetic and involved—spend much of their time doing social work and find it almost impossible to spare staff for trips to the swimming baths, and to keep staff who are willing or able to organise extra-curricular activities.

This report is not concerned, therefore, with making the point that some schools are 'good' in that they offer certain opportunities for physical recreation to their pupils and other schools are 'bad' because they offer fewer such opportunities. It is interested in the extent to which such variations in provision affect the lasting interest that children have in physical recreation. No answer to that question will be available until the follow-up interviews have been conducted and analysed. At this stage an attempt has been made to see if there is a connection between provision in school and sport-loving scores of children in their last year at school.

Tables 26(a) and (b) show schools ranked in order of the mean percentages of girls and then of boys in their last year who were seen in them, who said they did not hike, did not swim, did not do gym, and did not do athletics with the school, and the percentage of girls and of boys in each of these schools who scored over 11 on the sport-loving index and therefore fall into the very sport-loving category; and the percentage of girls and boys in each of these schools who scored under 6 on the sport-loving index and therefore fall into the non-sport-loving category.

It is clear from tables 26(a) and (b) that there is a great variation in provision between secondary modern schools in the sample. In some schools it was possible for a very high proportion of school leavers to say they had no current school experience of these four activities.

It is not easy to see from tables 26(a) and (b) whether or not there is a relationship between percentages from a school who took part in hiking, swimming, athletics and gymnastics with the school and the percentages of girls and boys in that school who were shown, by their answers to other questions, to be sport-loving. For this reason Spearman's rank correlation coefficient was calculated.

For girls the relationship between the percentage not doing the four sports at school and the percentage who were very sport-loving, starting from low to high, is 0·38. This is a significant positive correlation at the 6 per cent level: that is, the chances of such a relationship occurring by chance are 6 in 100.

For girls the relationship between the percentage not doing the four sports at school and the percentage who were not sport-loving is 0·21 This is not a significant correlation.

For boys the relationship between the percentage not doing the four sports at school and the percentage who were very sport-loving, starting from low to high, is −0·29. This is not a significant correlation.

For boys the relationship between the percentage not doing the four sports at school and the percentage who were not sport-loving is −0·01. This is not a significant correlation.

TABLE 26(*a*)

Girls' secondary modern schools ranked by mean percentages of girls in each school who said they did not go hiking, go swimming, do athletics or do gymnastics with the school

Schools*	Mean %	Percentage of very sport-loving girls	Percentage of non-sport-loving girls	Number of girls questioned in school
AG	90.3	4.5	73.9	88
BG	70.3	4.7	56.5	85
CG	66.0	10.0	64.0	50
DG	65.2	0.0	61.1	18
EG	62.5	8.3	45.8	48
FG	60.7	9.5	61.9	21
GG	58.9	9.5	45.2	42
HG	58.1	16.9	49.3	71
IG	56.2	10.7	35.7	28
JG	55.8	11.8	55.9	34
KG	55.4	13.8	49.2	65
LG	54.2	10.2	50.8	59
MG	46.1	2.8	76.1	71
NG	43.9	21.2	36.4	33
OG	43.4	0.0	63.2	57
PG	42.2	3.4	75.9	29
QG	37.5	23.2	46.2	26
RG	37.0	11.5	41.0	78
SG	36.6	14.0	51.2	43

* Names of schools are omitted to avoid possible misuse of the data. Mixed schools are here treated as though they each comprised two single-sex schools.

TABLE 26(*b*)

Boys' secondary modern schools ranked by mean percentages of boys in each school who said they did not go hiking, go swimming, do athletics or do gymnastics with the school

Schools*	Mean %	Percentage of very sport-loving boys	Percentage of non-sport-loving boys	Number of boys questioned in school
AB	73.8	61.9	0.0	21
BB	73.6	64.8	9.3	54
CB	67.6	41.5	19.5	41
DB	65.7	35.5	24.2	62
EB	56.9	53.2	8.5	47
FB	55.8	56.9	20.0	65
GB	55.4	68.6	2.0	51
HB	52.3	43.2	18.2	44
IB	51.3	48.7	18.9	37
JB	50.7	35.5	19.7	76
KB	49.2	55.0	18.3	60
LB	47.5	62.5	10.0	80
MB	45.5	42.9	10.7	28
NB	44.4	57.5	5.0	40
OB	44.3	35.8	34.0	53
PB	39.2	35.3	15.7	51
QB	38.0	52.0	16.8	125
RB	34.9	46.5	7.0	43

* Names of schools are omitted to avoid possible misuse of the data. Mixed schools are here treated as though they each comprised two single-sex schools.

Tables 26(c) and (d) show schools ranked in order of the number of sports played at the school.[2] Heads were asked to give, and in every case did give, details of sports and games played and facilities existing at school. In most cases their picture confirms the picture shown in tables 26(a)–(d). At school AG, for instance, at the time when the questionnaire was administered, there was no Physical Education teacher and there had not been one at the school for a considerable time. However, in some cases the two sources of evidence did conflict. Sometimes this was because the Head was not fully up to date with events in every section of a growing school. Sometimes it was because, whilst plans were afoot for activities and perhaps activities had been offered to some pupils, the activities were not effectively offered, since most pupils were not aware of their availability or were for other reasons unable to participate in them. The source of all the figures in this report is the evidence of pupils, and it was felt appropriate in this case to use their evidence.

Tables 26(c) and (d) show that there is a great variation in the provision of a range of physical activities between secondary modern schools in the sample.

It is not easy to see from tables 26(c) and (d) whether or not there is a relationship between the numbers of sports done in a school, with the school, and the percentage of girls and boys in that school who were shown, by their answers to other questions, to be sport-loving. For this reason the Kendall rank correlation coefficient *tau*[3] was calculated.

For girls the relationship between the numbers of sports done in a school and the percentage who were very sport-loving, starting from low to high, as measured by Kendall's

[2] The number of sports played at each school is taken from the children's answer to the question 'What games and sports do you play at school (apart from the activities already mentioned on this page)?' Answers to this question were coded under thirty-two named sports, and any other sport mentioned was coded as 'other'. In the calculation of the tables 'other' was counted as one. Thus the maximum possible number of sports for any one school was thirty-three.

[3] Kendall's *tau* rather than Spearman's rank correlation coefficient was used because there were many ties in the number of sports done in schools, and the calculations were corrected for ties.

TABLE 26(c)

Girls' secondary modern schools ranked by the number of sports school leavers said were done with that school (from least to most)

Schools	Number of sports	Percentage of very sport-loving girls	Percentage of non-sport-loving girls	Number of girls questioned in school
AG	5	4.5	73.9	88
FG	5	9.5	61.9	21
DG	5	0.0	61.1	18
OG	6	0.0	63.2	57
IG	6	10.7	35.7	28
LG	7	10.2	50.8	59
BG	7	4.7	56.5	85
QG	7	23.2	46.2	26
PG	7	3.4	75.9	29
MG	8	2.8	76.1	71
KG	8	13.8	49.2	65
RG	8	11.5	41.0	78
GG	9	9.5	45.2	42
NG	9	21.2	36.4	33
SG	9	14.0	51.2	43
CG	9	10.0	64.0	50
HG	10	16.9	49.3	71
JG	11	11.8	55.9	34
EG	13	8.3	45.8	48

TABLE 26(d)

Boys' secondary modern schools ranked by the number of sports school leavers said were done with that school (from least to most)

Schools	Number of sports	Percentage of very sport-loving	Percentage of non-sport-loving	Number of boys questioned in school
CB	6	41.5	19.5	41
HB	6	43.2	18.2	44
AB	8	61.9	0.0	21
EB	8	53.2	8.5	47
NB	9	57.5	5.0	40
GB	10	68.6	2.0	51
MB	10	42.9	10.7	28
OB	11	35.8	34.0	53
FB	11	56.9	20.0	65
PB	11	35.3	15.7	51
LB	12	62.5	10.0	80
JB	12	35.5	19.7	76
KB	12	55.0	18.3	60
RB	12	46.5	7.0	43
DB	13	35.5	24.2	62
IB	13	48.7	18.9	37
BB	13	64.8	9.3	54
QB	14	52.0	16.8	125

tau, is 0·34. This is a significant correlation at the 5 per cent level: that is, the probability of such a relationship occurring by chance is 5 in 100.

For girls the relationship between the number of sports done in a school and the percentage who were not sport-loving, as measured by Kendall's *tau*, is 0·19. This is not a significant correlation.

For boys the correlation between the number of sports done in a school and the percentage of very sport-loving boys in that school, as measured by Kendall's *tau*, is – 0·01. This is not a significant correlation.

For boys the correlation between the number of sports done in school and the percentage of non-sport-loving boys in that school, as measured by Kendall's *tau*, is – 0·15. This is not a significant correlation.

Thus these figures show that there is some relationship between provision offered in schools and the degree of interest in sports which school leavers show in the case of girls, but there is no such relation in the case of boys. Provision is related to the numbers of girls who score high on the index of love of sport. Lack of provision is not related to the numbers of girls who score low on the index.

It is possible that boys' interest in sport is created and supported by social circles and pressures outside the school and that therefore boys are relatively unaffected by the range of provision or the frequency of physical recreation periods at school. In the case of girls the figures suggest that girls respond to a wide range of provision on the part of the school. Until the follow-up interviews are completed, however, it will not be possible to see whether the increased interest among girls from well provided schools will last beyond the years of school attendance.

Section I. *'With it-ness' and sport*

An index of 'with it-ness' was compiled on the basis of answers to questions listed in appendix 3. Achieved scores ranged from 0 to 18. Children were put into three groups as nearly equivalent in numbers as was possible, and the 620 children scoring 0–4 were classified as low scorers, the 1,163 scoring 5–8 were classified as middle scorers, and the 902 scoring 9 or over were classified as high scorers.

Girls are slightly more 'with it' than boys; the mean 'with it' score for girls was 8; the mean score for boys, 6. The median 'with it' score for girls was 9; the median score for boys, 6. Working class girls are more 'with it' than middle class girls, and secondary modern school girls more 'with it' than selective school girls. School differences among boys are not so marked; and class differences among boys hardly exist.

TABLE 27

Mean 'with it' score for each type of school

	Girls	Boys
Direct grant lay	4	4
Direct grant Church	6	5
Maintained grammar	7	6
Maintained technical	7	6
Secondary modern other	9	6
Secondary modern Church	9	6

TABLE 28

Mean 'with it' score for each social class of origin

	Girls	Boys
Registrar-General's class 1	6	5
Registrar-General's class 2	7	6
Registrar-General's class 3	9	6
Registrar-General's class 4	9	6
Registrar-General's class 5	8	6
Fathers' occupation not given	9	7

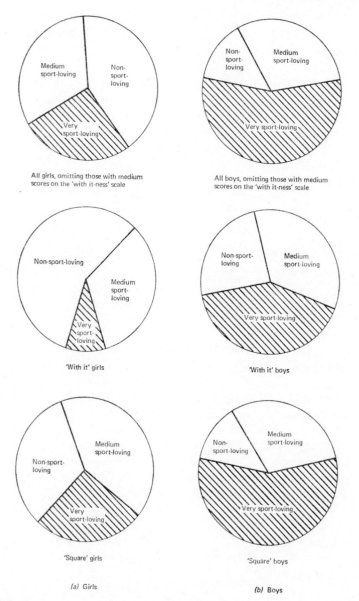

All girls, omitting those with medium
scores on the 'with it-ness' scale

All boys, omitting those with medium
scores on the 'with it-ness' scale

'With it' girls

'With it' boys

'Square' girls

'Square' boys

(a) Girls

(b) Boys

FIG. 4
Proportions of 'with it' and 'square' boys and girls who fall into three categories of sport-
loving, omitting those with medium scores on the 'with it-ness' scale

Tables 27 and 28 give mean 'with it' scores for girls and boys in different types of school and different social classes of origin.

TABLE 29

'With it-ness' and sport

	Low scorers (0 — 4)	Medium scorers (5 — 8)	High scorers (9+)	Total
	%	%	%	%
(a) All girls in the sample				
Non-sport-loving	32.4	46.1	56.5	49.5
Medium sport-loving	40.7	38.6	34.1	36.6
Very sport-loving	26.9	15.3	9.4	13.9
	100% = 182	100% = 438	100% = 649	100% = 1269
(b) All boys in the sample				
Non-sport-loving	13.0	11.7	24.9	14.5
Medium sport-loving	30.6	33.0	35.2	32.6
Very sport-loving	56.4	55.3	39.9	52.9
	100% = 438	100% = 725	100% = 253	100% = 1416

Table 29 shows each 'with it-ness' group divided into the sport-loving categories. The same data are shown pictorially in Fig. 4.

These tables give support to the seventh hypothesis, that 'cutting across class and age is what is here called a "with it-ness" factor, i.e. commitment to adolescent rather than adult values, and fewer "with it" youngsters will like sport than will other youngsters.' The picture is clouded by the far greater interest boys have in sport than have girls. Whether influenced by the adolescent sub-culture or not, most girls are not very sport-loving, but fewer 'with it' girls are sport-loving than 'square' girls.

Whether influenced by the adolescent sub-culture or not, most boys are sport-loving, but more 'square' boys are sport-loving than 'with it' boys.

Section J. *Sport and the solitary*

The eighth hypothesis suggested that children whose leisure activities centred on the home, and who spent more time with their family or alone than with friends, would tend to favour team rather than other sports. Clearly this is closely allied to commitment to adolescent or adult values, but it was thought it might be separable, and, as will be seen from appendices 2 and 3, different answers were used to score children for 'with it-ness' and for solitariness.

The index of solitariness was compiled on the basis of answers to questions listed in appendix 2. Achieved scores ranged from 0 to 21. Children were put into three groups as nearly equivalent in numbers as possible, and the 753 children scoring 0–7 were classified as gregarious; the 1,091 children scoring 8–11 were classified as medium, and the 841 children scoring 12 and over were classified as solitary or home-oriented.

The mean solitary score for girls was 10. The mean solitary score for boys was the same: 10. The median solitary score for girls was 10. The median solitary score for boys was 9.

The mean solitary score for each class of origin was:

RG 1	RG 2	RG 3	RG 4	RG 5	DK
11	10	10	9	10	9

The mean solitary score for each type of school was:

Direct grant Church	11
Direct grant lay	11
Maintained grammar	10
Maintained technical	10
Secondary modern lay	10
Secondary modern Church	9

Tables 30(*a*) and (*b*) show the percentage of gregarious, medium and solitary children who fall into the three categories of sport-loving for all boys and girls in the sample. Small proportions of each group of boys on this scale are non-sport-loving, but the solitary include a larger proportion of non-sport-loving

TABLE 30

Sport in relation to gregariousness

	Gregarious	Medium	Solitary
	%	%	%
(a) Girls			
Non-sport-loving	44.9	45.6	58.5
Medium sport-loving	38.9	37.2	33.7
Very sport-loving	16.2	17.2	7.8
	100% = 334	100% = 535	100% = 400
(b) Boys			
Non-sport-loving	12.2	10.3	22.0
Medium sport-loving	28.6	29.9	39.9
Very sport-loving	59.2	59.9	38.1
	100% = 419	100% = 556	100% = 441

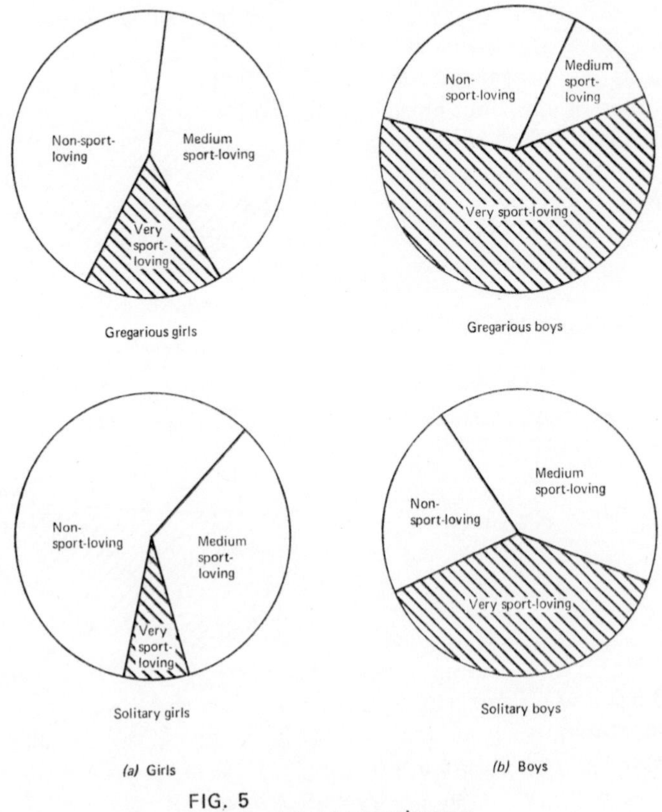

Gregarious girls

Gregarious boys

Solitary girls

Solitary boys

(a) Girls

(b) Boys

FIG. 5
Sport in relation to gregariousness

TABLE 31

Gregariousness and type of sport

	Team	Indoor	Outdoor	Equal indoor/ outdoor	Total
	%	%	%	%	
(a) *Girls*					
Gregarious	16.2	29.3	53.0	1.5	100% = 334
Medium	19.4	29.0	50.3	1.3	100% = 535
Solitary	27.2	35.0	36.5	1.3	100% = 400
(b) *Boys*					
Gregarious	41.5	35.1	23.2	0.2	100% = 419
Medium	43.3	34.7	21.8	0.2	100% = 556
Solitary	50.3	34.2	15.2	0.2	100% = 441

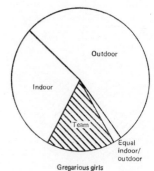

Gregarious girls

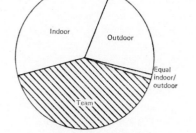

Gregarious boys

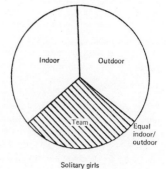

Solitary girls

Solitary boys

(a) Girls   *(b)* Boys

FIG. 6
Gregariousness and types of sport

67

boys than do the gregarious. Large proportions of each group of girls on this scale are non-sport-loving but the solitary include a larger proportion of non-sport-loving girls than do the gregarious. Thus there is a tendency for solitary boys and girls to be less interested in sport than are gregarious boys and girls. Fig. 5 shows some of these data pictorially.

Tables 31(a) and (b) show the types of sport preferred by gregarious, medium and solitary boys and girls. Figure 6 shows some of the same data pictorially.

From these figures it will be seen that, whether gregarious or solitary, most girls are predominantly interested in outdoor recreation, but more solitary girls than gregarious girls are predominantly interested in team sports. Whether gregarious or solitary, most boys are predominantly interested in team games. Thus some support is given to the eighth hypothesis, that more solitary or home-oriented children prefer team games than do gregarious children.[1]

---

[1] The conclusion that solitary or home-oriented children preferred organised team games more often than did gregarious children is one that caused surprise to some members of the team. It was possible that some distortion had occurred through categorising each child, whether he like or disliked sport as a whole, as preferring one type of sport.

A larger proportion of home-oriented children than of other children were non-sport-loving. The sports played in school are mainly team sports. Non-sport-loving children might be classified as predominantly interested in team sports because although the team/indoor/outdoor classification made hardly any use of sports done in school, that classification might be more strongly influenced by school sports in the case of non-sport-loving than in the case of sport-loving children. Thus it was possible that solitary children would look as though they preferred team sports when in fact the result really reflected their lack of interest in sport of any kind. This was not very likely, since had there been such a bias it is unlikely that a majority of girls would have been categorised as being predominantly interested in outdoor recreation, since girls are relatively uninterested in sport. However, the data in the above table were broken down and considered separately for each category of sport-loving.

In each case the proportion of solitary children preferring team sports was greater than the proportion of gregarious children preferring team sports.

Section K. *Locality and sport*

Comparisons between different parts of the conurbation have not been attempted yet, and there has not been time for even a provisional testing of the ninth hypothesis: that children living in parts of the conurbation relatively well provided with facilities for recreation will be more likely to take an active interest in sport and to continue with such an interest than those from poorly provided districts.

Section L. *Profiles*

There have been many indices in the results of the differences between the sport-loving child and the non-sport-loving child. Here an attempt is made to sketch out profiles.

The fact that social class is associated more strongly with interest in sport in the case of girls than of boys is reflected in other results. Thus, for instance, sport-loving children have more spending money than non-sport-loving children. The difference is minute in the case of boys but large in the case of girls. But a third of very sport-loving girls are middle class, so that the spending money reflects the fact that middle class children have more spending money than working class children. Thus differences between sport-loving and non-sport-loving boys are more likely to be connected with their interest in sport than are such differences between girls.

The very sport-loving child goes more often on holiday without his family, and when he[1] goes on such holidays stays more often in a caravan, hostel or camping than does the non-sport-loving child. He has more often been to the countryside with the school and this difference is particularly marked in the case of the sport-loving girl. He more often belongs to clubs in school, and out of school, apart from sports clubs, and this difference is much more marked among girls than among boys.

The first question on the questionnaire asked:

'Write down the three things you like doing best—that is, in the time after school.'

Table 32[2] shows the most popular activities and how they distinguish between the sport-loving and the non-sport-loving

[1] In the following discussion, 'he' is used as the personal pronoun for a boy or a girl, but differences in results for boys and girls are shown.

[2] An attempt has been made to exclude active sport from the table of which this chart is an extract. However, attending youth clubs and being out with friends will include some active participation in sport. Percentages are percentages, not of the number of children in each sport-loving category, but of the number of activities, other than active sports, mentioned by children in each category.

child. All the children in the sample were asked to say what they did and who they were with during each hourly period between 4 p.m. and 11 p.m. on the evening before the questionnaire was administered; and in the morning, afternoon and evening of the previous Saturday and Sunday.

TABLE 32(a)

Some favourite leisure activities for three sport-loving categories: girls

	Non-sport-loving	Medium sport-loving	Very sport-loving
	%	%	%
Dancing	16.4	21.3	22.1
Out with friends	12.8	11.5	14.1
Reading, writing, drawing	10.6	12.8	14.1
Cinema	11.6	10.4	7.1
Housework, drama, gardening and other non-sedentary hobbies	9.3	10.0	8.9
Television	9.6	9.0	3.7
Listening to popular music at home	9.9	5.6	4.6
Attending youth clubs, guides, etc.	6.6	7.7	10.7
Miscellaneous ie shopping, baby-sitting, preparing to go out, hanging about, spare time job, etc	6.0	4.7	6.7
Coffee clubs and beat clubs	4.3	2.9	3.4
Animal care	0.9	1.1	0.9

TABLE 32(b)

Some favourite leisure activities for three sport-loving categories: boys

	Non-sport-loving	Medium sport-loving	Very-sport-loving
	%	%	%
Out with friends	17.0	15.6	20.1
Reading, writing, drawing	13.5	12.2	10.4
Watching television	11.5	11.5	8.6
Gardening, housework, drama and other non-sedentary hobbies	9.7	10.7	8.3
Cinema	8.4	9.8	9.5
Attending youth clubs, cadets etc.	4.7	8.6	10.2
Miscellaneous i.e. shopping, part-time job, hanging about	5.7	6.3	5.5
Listening to popular music at home	6.9	4.6	3.2
Attending coffee clubs and beat clubs	5.1	3.5	4.3
Watching soccer	0.7	2.6	6.6
Driving a car or motor bike	4.2	4.0	3.8

The non-sport-loving boy more often spent time at home, at a cinema or club or engaged in miscellaneous activities outside the house than did the sport-loving boy. The non-sport-loving girl more often spent time at home or engaged in miscellaneous activities outside the home than did the very sport-loving girl, but all categories of girls spent the same amount of time going to clubs or the cinema.

Of all the boys in the sample, 72 per cent had bicycles compared with 42 per cent of all the girls, and more sport-loving children had bicycles than did non-sport-loving children.

Children were asked:

'Since they left school, have either of your parents taken an active part in a sport, game or outdoor activity at any time in their lives? If "Yes", please name the activities.'

Those answering 'Yes' fell into sport-loving categories as shown in table 33.

TABLE 33

Girls and boys in three sport-loving categories who knew of parents' active interest in sport

	Non-sport-loving	Medium sport-loving	Very sport-loving	Yes for all categories of sport-loving grouped together
Girls	29.0	42.7	65.1	40.2
Boys	30.0	39.6	55.6	47.3
Base for percentages:				
Girls	691	561	249	1501*
Boys	226	538	965	1729*

* The totals here are greater than the numbers of girls and boys in the sample because some children knew of sporting activities engaged in by both parents.

TABLE 34

Knowledge of parents' active interest in sport: all children in sample

Base for percentages	Girls 1501*	Boys 1729*
No	36.8	30.5
Do not know	22.8	22.2
Mother played in fixed team sport	1.9	1.6
Father played in fixed team sport	10.6	17.5
Mother played in other sport	12.6	11.7
Father played in other sport	15.1	16.5
Blank	0.2	0.1

* The totals here are greater than the numbers of girls and boys in the sample because some children knew of sporting activities engaged in by both parents.

The actual activities known by children to have been done by their parents were divided crudely into sports played by teams of fixed numbers and other sports. The results for all girls and all boys are shown in table 34.

More sport-loving girls and boys went out on many evenings than did non-sport-loving children in the week before they were questioned (see table 35).

TABLE 35

Numbers of evenings out in three sport-loving categories

	Non-sport-loving %	Medium sport-loving %	Very sport-loving %
(a) Girls			
Out none, one or two evenings	32.7	23.1	17.6
Out three or four evenings	37.2	42.7	39.6
Out five, six or seven evenings	30.0	34.3	42.9
	100% = 628	100% = 464	100% = 177
(b) Boys			
Out none, one or two evenings	32.7	28.6	18.9
Out three or four evenings	30.7	38.7	36.3
Out five, six or seven evenings	36.6	32.7	44.8
	100% = 205	100% = 462	100% = 749

Section M. *Conclusion*

The publicised provision of good facilities or the lack of or general ignorance of good facilities can, over some period of time, contribute to a situation where more or fewer people participate in any one physical activity. To a certain extent, supply creates demand and therefore the magnitude or lack of existing demand is not alone an adequate ground on which to base decisions about the supply of facilities. Thus this enquiry is not seen solely as an attempt to measure demand. The extent to which the publicised provision of good facilities is followed by increased participation varies in different sections of society and from sport to sport. Demand is changing constantly and at different speeds and in different ways and directions among different sections of society. Many studies and many different approaches are needed for a full understanding of the situation.

This enquiry concentrates on the life crisis which occurs to an individual at the age of leaving school and the changes in leisure activities which occur at this time. School leavers are not a homogeneous category, nor are school leavers in the south-east Lancashire conurbation a homogeneous category. They are divided by the forces that divide a society at large. An attempt has been made, therefore, to look at the divisions between school leavers which are significant in making an assessment of demand for facilities. Such divisions are themselves factors which affect the extent to which the leisure pattern of teenagers includes physical recreation, and these and other factors have been looked at in the first stage of the enquiry.

Fewer girls than boys are interested in active sport. This may be interpreted as meaning that there is little demand from girls and therefore little need for supply; or it may be interpreted as meaning that special efforts must be made to encourage a growth in demand from girls. In a similar way policy makers can make different uses of the other results reported herein. Here they are simply summarised.

One-third of the children in the sample said that after leaving school they would carry on with no sport, game or outdoor activity.

More girls are interested in outdoor recreation than are interested in team sports or indoor sports and games.

More boys are interested in team sports than are interested in indoor sports and games or outdoor recreation.

More middle class children than working class children are interested in active sport, and this is particularly marked in the case of girls. More children attending selective schools than those attending unselective schools are interested in active sport. More middle class children than working class children are actively interested in indoor sports and games.

Children who are committed to adolescent values are less interested in sport than children who are committed to adult values.

Solitary or home-oriented children are more often interested in team games than are gregarious children.

There is a correlation between the provision for physical recreation for girls in a school and the proportion of girls in their last year at that school who are very interested in active sport. The same is not true of boys. Whether or not the love of sport found in girls from well provided schools will persist after leaving school must be enquired into in the follow-up.

For girls, tennis, ten pin bowling, ice skating, table tennis, horse riding, rounders, badminton and athletics are middle class sports, in the sense that they were played more by that group in free time out of school, whilst netball, gymnastics, bowling on a green and hockey are working class sports.

Badminton, when played at school as part of the school timetable, was liked by a majority in all groups of girls, including those who were not interested in active sport.

Tennis, badminton, volleyball, when played at school as part of the school timetable, were liked by girls with only a medium interest in active sport as well as by those very interested in active sport.

For boys, tennis, golf, fishing, ice skating, ten pin bowling, table tennis and cricket are middle class sports, whilst soccer, rugby and athletics are working class sports.

Tennis, when played at school as part of the school timetable, was liked by a majority of each group of boys, including those who were not interested in active sport. Tennis, basketball and badminton, when played at school as part of the school time-table, were liked by boys with only a medium interest in active sport as well as by those very interested in active sport. Cross-country running and cricket, when played at school as part of the school timetable, were unpopular with a majority of all groups of boys. Out of school, cricket was popular, but cross-country running was not.

When children gave reasons why they did not do certain sports that they would like to, lack of accessible facilities was the reason most often given, with expense being cited by some in the case of outdoor recreation and lack of training being cited by some in the case of team sports.

Appendix 1

Questions and answers used to score on 'love of sport' index

PART ONE OF THE QUESTIONNAIRE

1. Write down the three things you like doing best—that is, in the time after school. [If *one* of the answers was a sport, *one* point was given. If *two* of the answers were sports, *two* points were given. If *three* of the answers were sports, *three* points were given.]

2. Here is a list of places to spend your time. Which would you like most to have within easy reach of your home? Please read them through and then number them in order, putting a 1 by the side of the place that interests you most, a 2 by the place that interests you next, and so on.

   Swimming pool
   Club where pop groups appear
   Public library
   Cinema
   Playing field or recreation ground
   Theatre
   Club where you can play indoor games and sports
   Dance hall
   Concert hall or art gallery

   [If 'playing field' was included in the first three choices, *one* point was given. If 'Club where you can play indoor games and sports' was included in the first three choices, *one* point was given.]

3. If you could have any job you wanted when you left school, or finished full-time education, what job would you choose? WRITE THE ANSWER. [If the dream job given was connected with active sport, *one* point was given.]

6. Tick which one you would most like to be. TICK ONE ONLY.
[*Wording for boys*]	[*Wording for girls*]
Businessman	Wife of businessman
League footballer	Tennis champion

77

Pop singer   Pop singer
Scientist   Teacher
Doctor working in Africa   Nurse working in Africa

[If 'League footballer' or 'Tennis champion' was ticked, *one* point was given.]

11. What are your *two* favourite regular TV programmes? WRITE THE ANSWER. [If *one* of the programmes given was about sport, *one* point was given. If *two* of the programmes given were about sport *two* points were given.]

16. Do you belong to any kind of club or organisation *in school* or to a group which stays on at school after lessons? TICK THE CORRECT ANSWER. Yes .... No .... If 'Yes', name the club, organisation or group and say what you do there:

Name of club	*What you do*
....	....
....	....
....	....

[If *one* sports club was named, *one* point was given. If *two* sports clubs were named *two* points were given. If *three* sports clubs were named, *three* points were given.]

17. Do you belong to any kind of club or organisation *out of school* apart from those already mentioned? TICK THE CORRECT ANSWER. Yes .... No .... If 'Yes', name the club or organisation and say what you do there:

Name of club	*What you do*
....	....
....	....
....	....

[If *one* sports club[1] was named, *one* point was given. If *two* sports clubs were named, *two* points were given. If *three* sports clubs were named, *three* points were given.]

19. Have you a hobby? TICK THE CORRECT ANSWER. Yes .... No .... If 'Yes', name it: .... [If a sport was given as a hobby, *one* point was given.]

[1] At which the respondent participated in a sport.

26. What did you do, and who were you with, between finishing lessons at school and going to bed yesterday? WRITE DOWN THE ANSWER.

	What did you do?	Who with?
From 4–5 p.m.	....	....
From 5–6 p.m.	....	....
From 6–7 p.m.	....	....
From 7–8 p.m.	....	....
From 8–9 p.m.	....	....
From 9–10 p.m.	....	....
After 10 p.m.	....	....

27. What did you do, and who were you with, last Saturday? WRITE DOWN THE ANSWER.

	What did you do?	Who with?
Morning	....	....
Afternoon	....	....
Evening	....	....

28. What did you do, and who were you with, last Sunday? WRITE DOWN THE ANSWER.

	What did you do?	Who with?
Morning	....	....
Afternoon	....	....
Evening	....	....

[If active participation in team sports was recorded in the 'recall diary', *one* point was given. If active participation in indoor games and sport was recorded in the 'recall diary', *one* point was given. If active participation in outdoor activities was recorded in the 'recall diary', *one* point was given.]

[Total of three points possible for these questions.]

29. Last summer, on Saturdays and Sundays in term time, what did you spend most of your spare time doing? THINK, AND THEN WRITE DOWN THE ANSWER.

30. Last summer, in the weekdays after school, what did you spend most of your spare time doing? THINK, AND THEN WRITE DOWN THE ANSWER.

31. Last summer, in the school holidays, what did you spend most of your spare time doing? THINK, AND THEN WRITE DOWN THE ANSWER.

32. This winter, on Saturdays and Sundays in term time, what did you spend most of your spare time doing? THINK, AND THEN WRITE DOWN THE ANSWER.

33. This winter, in the weekdays after school, what did you spend most of your spare time doing? THINK, AND THEN WRITE DOWN THE ANSWER.

34. This winter, in the holidays, what did you spend most of your spare time doing? THINK, AND THEN WRITE DOWN THE ANSWER.

[If active participation in team sports was recorded in these questions, *one* point was given. If active participation in indoor games and sports was recorded in these questions, *one* point was given. If active participation in outdoor activities (such as water sports, camping, tennis, cycling) was recorded in these questions, *one* point was given. If active participation in miscellaneous outdoor activities (such as fishing, farming, walks in the country) was recorded in these questions, *one* point was given.]

[Total of four points possible for these questions]

PART TWO OF THE QUESTIONNAIRE

11. Do you go swimming apart from when you go with or for the school? TICK THE CORRECT ANSWER. Yes .... No .... If 'Yes', how often? .... [If the answer was coded as 'Yes, often', *two* points were given. If the answer was coded as 'Yes, seldom', *one* point was given.]

12. Do you go hiking or rambling apart from when you go with or for the school? TICK THE CORRECT ANSWER. Yes .... No .... If 'Yes', how often? .... [If the answer was coded as 'Yes, often', *two* points were given. If the answer was coded as 'Yes, seldom', *one* point was given.]

13. What games, sports, athletics or gymnastics do you take part in *apart from* those you take part in with or for the school? WRITE DOWN THEIR NAMES, AND HOW OFTEN YOU DO THEM, AND WHO WITH (i.e. with a team or club, or with a few friends). If none, write 'None'.

Name of sport or activity	*How often?*	*Who with?*
....	....	....
....	....	....

[For each sport coded as being played 'often', *two* points were given (answers coded under 34 sports and 'other'). For each sport coded as 'not often' *one* point was given.]

14. Are you in any school team? TICK THE CORRECT ANSWER. Yes .... No .... If 'Yes', for what? ....
[If a member of a team playing a game with a fixed number in the team playing against another team, such as football, cricket, rounders, *one* point was given. If a member of a team playing another game, such as table tennis, judo, canoeing, swimming, *one* point was given. Two points possible for this answer.]

15. Are you in any team outside school? TICK THE CORRECT ANSWER. Yes .... No .... If 'Yes', for what?...................
[Points given as for question 14.]

19. What main sport, game or outdoor activity do you think you'll do AFTER you leave school or college? WRITE THE ANSWER. IF YOU ARE UNLIKELY TO DO ANY, WRITE 'NONE'. [If any sport was named, *one* point was given.]

20. Are you a person who plays sports and games at school but NOT in your own spare time? TICK THE CORRECT ANSWER. Yes .... No .... [If the answer was 'No', *one* point was given.]

Appendix 2

Questions and answers used to score on 'solitary or home-loving/ gregarious' index

Each child was given eleven points to start with.

1. Write down the three things you like doing best—that is, in the time after school. [Of stamp collecting, reading, writing, drawing, playing cards, or other sedentary hobbies, gardening, drama, housework, or animal care, if one was mentioned in the answer, *one* point was given; if two were mentioned, *two* points were given; if three were mentioned, *three* points were given. Of cinema, youth clubs or going out with friends, if one was mentioned in the answer, *one* point was subtracted; if two were mentioned, *two* points were subtracted; if three were mentioned, *three* points were subtracted.]

2. Here is a list of places to spend your time. Which would you like most to have within easy reach of your home? Please read them through and then number them in order, putting a 1 by the side of the place that interests you most, a 2 by the place that interests you next, and so on.

> Swimming pool
> Club where pop groups appear
> Public library
> Cinema
> Playing field or recreation ground
> Theatre
> Club where you can play indoor games and sports
> Dance hall
> Concert hall or art gallery

[If 'Library' was included in the first three choices, *one* point was given.]

13. Do you go regularly to a club or cafe to listen to or dance to pop music? TICK THE CORRECT ANSWER. Yes .... No ....
IF 'YES', WRITE NAME OR NAMES OF CLUBS.   HOW OFTEN DO YOU GO?
....

82

14. Do you go regularly to a dance hall? TICK THE CORRECT ANSWER. Yes ...... No .... If 'Yes', how often? ....
[If the answer was 'No' to *both* these questions, *one* point was given.]

18. Apart from those already mentioned, do you have a regular place to go outside your home, where you meet a friend or friends? Yes .... No .... If 'Yes', name it : ....
[If the answer was 'No', *one* point was given. If the answer was 'Yes, a club, cafe, pub, cinema, park, church, rink, or shop', *one* point was subtracted.]

19. Have you a hobby? TICK THE CORRECT ANSWER. Yes .... No .... If 'Yes', name it .... [If the answer was 'Yes' and named a sedentary hobby likely to be carried on alone, such as stamp collecting, making models, reading, *one* point was given.]

26. What did you do, and who were you with, between finishing lessons at school and going to bed yesterday? WRITE DOWN THE ANSWER.

What did you do?	*Who with?*
From 4–5 p.m.	....
From 5–6 p.m.	....
From 6–7 p.m.	....
From 7–8 p.m.	....
From 8–9 p.m.	....
From 9–10 p.m.	....
After 10 p.m.	....

27. What did you do, and who were you with, last Saturday? WRITE DOWN THE ANSWER.

What did you do?	*Who with?*
Morning	....
Afternoon	....
Evening	....

28. What did you do, and who were you with, last Sunday? WRITE DOWN THE ANSWER.

What did you do?	*Who with?*
Morning	....
Afternoon	....
Evening	....

[If seventeen hours or over were spent at home, *one* point was given. If most hours were spent with family, or alone, or an equal number of hours was spent with family and alone, *one* point was given. If most hours were spent with friends, *one* point was substracted.]

36. Did you go away from home without your family during your last summer holiday? TICK THE CORRECT ANSWER. Yes .... No........... If 'Yes', WHERE DID YOU GO? Tick the correct answer:

> Countryside in Great Britain
> Inland town in Great Britain
> Abroad
> Touring in Great Britain
> Seaside in Great Britain
> Other (name it)

AND WHERE DID YOU STAY? Tick the correct answer:

> Lodgings, bed and breakfast or hotel
> Rented cottage or house
> With friends or relations
> Holiday camp
> Camping
> Slept in car
> Youth hostel
> Caravan

AND WHO DID YOU GO WITH? Write answer ....
[If the answer was 'Yes, went with a friend or several friends', *one* point was subtracted.]

38. Do you spend most of your spare time with (TICK ONE ONLY):

> a girl friend
> a boy friend
> your family
> a group of boys
> a group of girls
> a group of boys and girls
> adults outside your family

[If 'family' was ticked or 'alone' written, *one* point was given. If friend of same sex or any group of friends was ticked, *one* point was subtracted.]

43. When did you last go to the pictures? TICK THE CORRECT ANSWER.

> Within the last week
> Over a week ago but less than a month ago
> Over a month ago
> I almost never or never go
> Don't know

[If 'Within the last week' or 'Over a week but less than a month' was ticked, *one* point was subtracted.]

45. Last week, did you spend most of the evening *at home* or *out* on the following days? TICK THE CORRECT ANSWER FOR EACH DAY:

	Spent most of the evening *at* home	Spent most of the evening out
Monday	....	....
Tuesday	....	....
Wednesday	....	....
Thursday	....	....
Friday	....	....
Saturday	....	....
Sunday	....	....

[Half a point was subtracted for each of the following days if *out* was ticked: Monday or Tuesday or Wednesday or Thursday or Sunday; and a quarter of a point was subtracted if *out* was ticked for Friday or Saturday. A maximum of three points could be subtracted.]

49. Suppose your parents had planned a trip for the whole family for a Saturday and your friends asked you to go out with them on the same Saturday. Your parents can't change their plans but leave it up to you to go with them or with your friends. What do you think you would do—go with your friends or with your family? TICK THE CORRECT ANSWER.

> With my family ....
> With my friends ....

[If 'family' was ticked, *one* point was given.]

Appendix 3

Questions and answers used to score on 'with it-ness' index (index of commitment to adolescent values)

Each child was given two points to start with.

1. Write down the three things you like doing best—that is, in the time after school. [If the answer included listening to popular music at home, and dancing, *two* points were given; if it included one of these, *one* point was given.]

2. Here is a list of places to spend your time. Which would you most like to have within easy reach of your home? Please read them through and then number them in order, putting a 1 by the side of the place that interests you most, a 2 by the place that interests you next, and so on:

   Swimming pool
   Club where pop groups appear
   Public library
   Cinema
   Playing field or recreation ground
   Theatre
   Club where you can play indoor games and sports
   Dance hall
   Concert hall or art gallery

   [If 'Club where pop groups appear' and 'Dance hall' were included in the first three choices, *two* points were given; if one of these was included, *one* point was given. If 'Theatre' was included in the first three choices, *one* point was subtracted.]

6. Tick which one you would most like to be. TICK ONE ONLY.

[*Wording for boys*]	[*Wording for girls*]
Businessman	Wife of businessman
League footballer	Tennis champion
Pop singer	Pop singer
Scientist	Teacher
Doctor working in Africa	Nurse working in Africa

   [If 'Pop singer' was ticked, *one* point was given.]

7. If you could have chosen to leave school at any age you wanted, at what age would you have decided to leave? Write an age: .... [If 14 or under was the age mentioned, *one* point was given.]

8. Are you engaged or going steady with a girl/boy? TICK THE CORRECT ANSWER. Yes .... No .... [If 'Yes', *one* point was given.]

9. What do you think is a good age for a boy/girl to marry? Write an age: .... [If 19 or under, *one* point was given.]

13. Do you go regularly to a club or cafe to listen to or dance to pop music? TICK THE CORRECT ANSWER. Yes .... No .... IF 'YES', WRITE NAME OR NAMES OF CLUBS. HOW OFTEN DO YOU GO? ....
[If commercial beat club attended once a week or more often, *one* point was given. If other club attended once a week or more often, *one* point was given.]

14. Do you go regularly to a dance hall? TICK THE CORRECT ANSWER. Yes .... No .... If 'Yes', how often? ....
[If answer was 'Yes, once a week, or more often', *one* point was given.]

16. Do you belong to any kind of club or organisation *in school* or to a group which stays on at school after lessons? TICK THE CORRECT ANSWER. Yes .... No .... IF 'YES', NAME THE CLUB, ORGANISATION OR GROUP AND SAY WHAT YOU DO THERE:

Name of club	*What you do*
....	....

[If a club for chess, debate, drama, language, photography, art, music, charity or religion was mentioned, *one* point was subtracted.]

26. What did you do, and who were you with, between finishing lessons at school and going to bed yesterday? WRITE DOWN THE ANSWER.

	What did you do?	*Who with?*
From 4–5 p.m.	....	....
From 5–6 p.m.	....	....
From 6–7 p.m.	....	....

From 7–8 p.m. ....
From 8–9 p.m. ....
From 9–10 p.m. ....
After 10 p.m. ....

27. What did you do, and who were you with, last Saturday?
WRITE DOWN THE ANSWER.

What did you do?	*Who with?*
Morning	....
Afternoon	....
Evening	....

28. What did you do, and who were you with, last Sunday?
WRITE DOWN THE ANSWER.

What did you do?	*Who with?*
Morning	....
Afternoon	....
Evening	....

[If cinema or clubs were mentioned in the diary, *one* point
was given.]

38. Who do you spend most of your spare time with (TICK ONE
ONLY)?

    A girl friend
    A boy friend
    Your family
    A group of boys
    A group of girls
    A group of girls and boys
    Adults outside your family

[If friend of the opposite sex ticked, *one* point was given.]

39. What comics did you read last week? WRITE NAME OF COMIC(S)
OR 'NONE'. [If one or more teenage fashion, film or pop comics,
such as *Jackie, Romeo, Mirabelle, Boyfriend, Valentine, Rave* or
Princess were named, *one* point was given.]

40. What magazines did you read last week? WRITE NAME OF
MAGAZINE(S) OR 'NONE'. [If one or more teenage pop or fashion
magazines, such as *Petticoat, Trend, Honey, Fabulous, New
Musical Express, Music Parade, Annabel, Elvis Monthly* or
Stones Monthly, one point was given.]

44. Sometimes when a pupil is doing particularly well the teacher asks this pupil to be an assistant in the class. If you were chosen and the job did not involve any extra time at school how would you feel about it? TICK THE CORRECT ANSWER:

> I would like to be chosen ....
> I wouldn't like to be chosen ....

[If 'I wouldn't like to be chosen' was ticked, *one* point was given.]

47. How many records have you bought in the last month, and what were they? WRITE DOWN THE NUMBER AND NAMES. IF NONE, WRITE 'NONE'. Number: .... Names: ....

[If more than two records bought, *one* point was given.]

48. If you had the money to buy any record you liked for yourself, what would you buy? WRITE DOWN THE NAME OF THE SONG, TUNE OR PIECE OF MUSIC *AND* THE GROUP OR ORCHESTRA YOU WOULD LIKE. [If a piece of popular music was named, *one* point was given.]

PART TWO OF THE QUESTIONNAIRE

20. Are you a person who plays sports and games at school but *not* in your own spare time? TICK THE CORRECT ANSWER.
Yes .... No ....
If 'Yes', could you write down briefly why you don't do sports in your own spare time?
....

If you don't play sports and games in your spare time, could you write down what sort of things you prefer to do, and why?
....

[If the answer was 'Yes, I prefer going to clubs, listening to records, dancing, etc., *one* point was given.]

Note. These were the questions and answers that remained on the index after item discrimination tests had been used on questions which, on face value, appeared to indicate adherence to adolescent values. Thus, for instance, in question 47 it was not assumed that those who bought two or more records in a week bought popular music. There was a significant positive correlation between those who said they had bought two or more records and those who scored high on the crude 'with it-ness' index.

Appendix 4

Questions and answers used to score on 'types of sport' index

1. Write down the three things you like doing best—that is, in the time after school. [*One outdoor* point was given for *each* of the following answers: horse riding, swimming, cycling, boating, tennis, hiking, climbing, walking, pot-holing, camping, shooting, bird watching, bird nesting. *One team* point was given for *each* of the following answers: cricket, netball, soccer, rugby, hockey, other team sports. *One indoor* point was given for *each* of the following answers: ice skating, roller skating, boxing, judo, weight-lifting, wrestling, ten pin bowling, and other games and sports which can be done with any number.]

16. Do you belong to any kind of club or organisation *in school* or to a group which stays on at school after lessons? TICK THE CORRECT ANSWER. Yes .... No..........

    IF 'YES', NAME THE CLUB, ORGANISATION OR GROUP AND SAY WHAT YOU DO THERE:

Name of club	What you do
....	....

    [*One outdoor* point was given for *each* club mentioned in the answer pertaining to outdoor activities or water sports. *One team* point was given for *each* club mentioned pertaining to the common team sports, to athletics or to cross-country running. *One indoor* point was given for *each* club mentioned pertaining to indoor games such as skating, ten pin bowling, table tennis, keep fit, judo, etc. No more than three clubs were coded.]

26. What did you do, and who were you with, between finishing lessons at school and going to bed yesterday? WRITE DOWN THE ANSWER:

What did you do?	*Who with?*
From 4–5 p.m.	....
From 5–6 p.m.	....
From 6–7 p.m.	....
From 7–8 p.m.	....
From 8–9 p.m.	....
From 9–10 p.m.	....
After 10 p.m.	....

27. What did you do, and who were you with, last Saturday? WRITE DOWN THE ANSWER.

What did you do?	*Who with?*
Morning	....
Afternoon	....
Evening	....

28. What did you do, and who were you with, last Sunday? WRITE DOWN THE ANSWER.

What did you do?	*Who with?*
Morning	....
Afternoon	....
Evening	....

[*One outdoor* point was given for a mention of an outdoor activity/ies in the diary. *One team* point was given for a mention of a team sport(s) in the diary. *One indoor* point was given for a mention of an indoor game(s) in the diary.]

29. Last summer, on Saturdays and Sundays in term time, what did you spend most of your spare time doing? THINK, AND THEN WRITE DOWN THE ANSWER.

30. Last summer, in the weekdays after school, what did you spend most of your spare time doing? THINK, AND THEN WRITE DOWN THE ANSWER.

31. Last summer, in the school holidays, what did you spend most of your spare time doing? THINK, AND THEN WRITE DOWN THE ANSWER.

32. This winter, on Saturdays and Sundays in term time, what did you spend most of your spare time doing? THIINK, AND THEN WRITE DOWN THE ANSWER.

33. This winter, in the weekdays after school, what did you spend most of your spare time doing? THINK, AND THEN WRITE DOWN THE ANSWER.

34. This winter, in the holidays, what did you spend most of your spare time doing? THINK, AND THEN WRITE DOWN THE ANSWER.

[One outdoor point was given for a mention of an outdoor activity/ies. One team point was given for a mention of a team game/s. One indoor point was given for a mention of an indoor game/s.]

PART TWO OF THE QUESTIONNAIRE

7. Do you do gymnastics at school? TICK THE CORRECT ANSWER. Yes .... No .... If 'Yes', do you like it? Yes .... No .... [One indoor point was given if the answer was 'Yes' to both sections of the question.]

8. Do you do athletics at school? TICK THE CORRECT ANSWER. Yes .... No .... If 'Yes' do you like it? Yes .... No .... [One team point was given if the answer to both sections was 'Yes'.]

9. Do you go hiking or rambling with the school? TICK THE CORRECT ANSWER. Yes .... No .... If 'Yes', do you like it? Yes .... No .... [One outdoor point was given if the answer was 'Yes' to both sections of the question.]

13. What games, sports, athletics or gymnastics do you take part in apart from those you take part in with or for the school? WRITE DOWN THEIR NAMES AND HOW OFTEN YOU DO THEM, AND WHO WITH (i.e. with a team or club, or with a few friends). If none, write 'None':

Name of sport or activity	How often?	Who with?
....	....	....
....	....	....

[*One outdoor* point was given for *each* mention of an outdoor activity, whether often or seldom participated in. *One team* point was given for *each* mention of a team activity, whether often or seldom participated in. *One indoor* point was given for *each* mention of an indoor game, whether often or seldom participated in.]

17. Are there any other sports, games or outdoor activities which you don't play regularly but which you have thought of taking up regularly if you had the chance? TICK THE CORRECT ANSWER. Yes .... No .... If 'Yes', write down their names and the reasons why you don't play them:

Name	*Why you don't play them*
....	....
....	....

[*One outdoor* point was given for *each* mention of an outdoor activity. *One team* point was given for *each* mention of a team game. *One indoor* point was given for *each* mention of an indoor game.]

18. Here is a list. WILL YOU PLEASE READ IT, AND IF YOU HAVE DONE ANY OF THESE THINGS IN THE PAST YEAR, PLEASE TICK THEM IN THE CORRECT COLUMN ACCORDING TO WHETHER YOU HAVE WATCHED THEM OR DONE THEM. If you have watched AND done any of them, tick both columns for that item.

THINGS DONE DURING THE PAST YEAR

Tick below if done yourself

National or folk dancing ....
Ballet or *competitive* ballroom dancing ....
Other kinds of dancing ....

	Tick below if:			Tick below if:	
	done it yourself	*attended as a spectator*		*done it yourself*	*attended as a spectator*
Swimming	....	....	Rugger	....	....
Soccer	....	....	Volleyball	....	....
Cricket	....	....	Netball	....	....
Hockey	....	....	Handball	....	....
Basketball	....	....	Tennis	....	....
Baseball	....	....	Lacrosse	....	....

	Tick below if: *done it yourself*	*attended as a spectator*		Tick below if: *done it yourself*	*attended as a spectator*
Squash	....	....	Surfing	....	....
Fives	....	....	Water ski-ing	....	....
Badminton	....	....	Aqua-lung		
Table tennis	....	....	diving	....	....
Golf	....	....	Sailing	....	....
Croquet	....	....	Rowing	....	....
Bowling			Canoeing	....	....
(on a green)	......	....	Boating	....	....
Bowling			Pleasure craft		
(ten pin)	....	....	cruising	....	....
Shooting			Boxing	....	....
(indoor)	....	....	Wrestling	....	....
Shooting (outdoor—			Weight-lifting	......	....
all kinds)	....	....	Judo or karate	......	....
Archery	....	....	Keep-fit classes	......	....
Fencing	....	....	Gymnastics	....	....
Bird watching	......	....	Athletics (track		
Horse riding	....	....	and field)	....	....
Pony trekking	......	....	Cross-country		
Hunting			running	....	....
(all kinds)	....	....	Mountaineering	......	....
Polo	....	....	Rock climbing	......	....
Horse racing	....	....	Pot-holing	....	....
Greyhound			Stock car		
racing	....	....	racing	....	....
Motor racing	......	....	Go-kart racing	......	....
Motor cycle			Bicycle racing	....	....
racing	....	....	Motor-cycle		
Ice skating	....	....	scrambles	....	....
Roller skating	....	....	Speedway		
Fishing	....	....	racing	....	....
Organised			Ski-ing	....	....
rambling	....	....	Amateur flying	......	....
			Gliding	....	....

[*One outdoor* point[1] was given for a tick by *each* of the following: swimming, tennis, golf, bowling on a green, shooting (out-

[1] The maximum possible score varied with each type of sport. Scores were made comparable by a conversion with Pearson's table 1.

94

door), archery, fishing, rambling, surfing, water ski-ing, aqua-lung diving, sailing, rowing, canoeing, boating, pleasure craft cruising, mountaineering, rock climbing, pot-holing, bird watching, horse riding, pony trekking, hunting, polo, go-karting, bicycle racing, ski-ing, flying, gliding. *One team* point was given for a tick by *each* of the following: soccer, rugby, cricket, hockey, basketball, baseball, volleyball, netball, handball, lacrosse, athletics, cross-country running. *One indoor* point was given for a tick by *each* of the following: folk dancing, ballroom dancing, squash, fives, badminton, table tennis, ten pin bowling, shooting (indoors), fencing, ice skating, roller skating, boxing, wrestling, judo, keep-fit, gymnastics, weight-lifting. Only ticks in the 'Done it yourself' column were used here.]

19. What main sport, game or outdoor activity do you think you'll do *after* you leave school or college? WRITE THE ANSWER. IF YOU ARE UNLIKELY TO DO ANY, WRITE 'NONE'. [*One outdoor* point was given for an outdoor activity reply. *One team* point was given for a team game reply. *One indoor* point was given for an indoor game reply.]

Appendix 5

Reasons school leavers give for not doing some activities

The children in the sample were asked: 'Are there any other sports, games or outdoor activities which you don't play regularly but which you have thought of taking up regularly if you had the chance? TICK THE CORRECT ANSWER. Yes .... No .... If "Yes", write down their names and the reasons why you don't play them.' Their answers are analysed by type of sport in tables 16(*a*) and (*b*). In tables 36–39 these answers are analysed for individual activities.

TABLE 36

Individual activities which school leavers would do but do not, analysed by reasons given: all who gave positive answers to this question from all schools

	Total		Friends will not	Facilities far or lacking/no space	Expense/no equipment	Training lacking	Too young	Cannot get in a team/not good enough/physique	Other
Judo	115	G 60	3	16	8	5	2	–	26
		B 55	1	15	10	3	–	–	26
Tennis	97	G 56	6	18	3	4	–	–	25
		B 41	5	10	6	–	–	1	19
Ten pin bowling	86	G 54	3	26	20	–	–	–	5
		B 32	–	17	13	–	–	–	2
Golf	80	G 13	1	2	2	1	–	2	5
		B 67	–	8	32	3	–	1	23
Ice skating	70	G 58	1	27	19	2	–	1	8
		B 12	–	6	4	–	–	–	2
Football	65	G 20	1	1	–	9	–	–	9
		B 45	3	7	2	3	–	8	22
Ski-ing	50	G 20	–	12	6	1	–	–	1
		B 30	–	20	9	–	–	–	1
Badminton	46	G 16	–	12	1	–	1	–	2
		B 30	1	19	2	–	1	–	7
Canoeing	46	G 17	2	11	2	–	–	–	2
		B 29	–	12	13	–	–	–	4
Horse riding	43	G 32	1	11	13	1	–	–	6
		B 11	–	3	7	1	–	–	–
Swimming	40	G 23	2	2	1	1	–	–	17
		B 17	2	1	–	2	–	2	10

	Total		Friends will not	Facilities far or lacking/no space	Expense/no equipment	Training lacking	Too young	Cannot get in a team/not good enough/physique	Other
Rugby	38	G 2	—	—	1	—	—	—	1
		B 36	5	10	—	3	1	1	16
Table tennis	36	G 14	—	8	2	—	—	--	4
		B 22	2	8	3	—	—	1	8
Sailing	35	G 18	1	11	4	—	—	—	2
		B 17	—	6	8	1	—	—	2
Rock climbing	31	G 9	—	6	1	—	—	—	2
		B 22	1	8	5	2	1	1	4
Netball	29	G 29	2	11	—	2	—	—	14
		B 0	—	—	—	—	—	—	—
Athletics	26	G 10	—	5	—	1	—	—	4
		B 16	—	7	—	—	—	1	8
Cricket	26	G 6	2	—	—	1	—	—	3
		B 20	3	1	2	3	—	1	10
Basketball	25	G 6	1	1	—	1	—	1	2
		B 19	—	9	—	1	—	4	5
Karate	22	G 3	—	1	—	—	—	—	2
		B 19	—	6	6	1	—	1	5
Go-kart	21	G 2	—	2	—	—	—	—	—
		B 19	—	9	10	—	—	—	—
Surfing	21	G 8	—	8	—	—	—	—	—
		B 13	—	11	2	—	—	—	—
Aqualung	20	G 6	1	2	2	—	—	—	1
		B 14	—	7	6	—	—	—	1
Fencing	20	G 9	—	6	—	—	—	—	3
		B 11	—	6	—	1	1	—	3
Water ski-ing	20	G 9	—	6	2	—	1	—	—
		B 11	—	9	—	—	—	—	2
Shooting	19	G 1	—	—	1	—	—	—	—
		B 18	—	9	3	—	2	—	4
Car racing/ rallying	18	G 1	—	—	—	—	1	—	—
		B 17	—	—	15	—	2	—	—
Snooker	18	G 0	—	—	—	—	—	—	—
		B 18	3	4	2	—	—	—	9
Hockey	17	G 13	2	3	3	—	—	2	3
		B 4	—	1	1	—	—	—	2
Motor cycle scrambling	17	G 0	—	—	—	—	—	—	—
		B 17	—	5	4	1	3	—	4
Rounders	16	G 16	—	6	3	—	—	—	7
		B 0	—	—	—	—	—	—	—

	Total			Friends will not	Facilities far or lacking/no space	Expense/no equipment	Training lacking	Too young	Cannot get in a team/not good enough/physique	Other
Squash	16	G	4	–	4	–	–	–	–	–
		B	12	–	6	4	1	–	–	1
Pot-holing	15	G	0	–	–	–	–	–	–	–
		B	15	4	5	2	–	–	–	4
Gymnastics	14	G	7	–	5	1	–	–	–	1
		B	7	1	2	–	1	–	–	3
Hiking	14	G	9	1	1	–	2	–	–	5
		B	5	–	–	–	–	–	–	5
Cycling	13	G	3	2	–	1	–	–	–	–
		B	10	–	–	5	–	–	–	5
Volleyball	12	G	4	–	2	–	–	–	–	2
		B	8	1	3	1	–	–	–	3
Yachting	11	G	4	–	2	2	–	–	–	–
		B	7	–	3	3	–	–	–	1
Archery	10	G	2	–	2	–	–	–	–	–
		B	8	–	4	3	–	–	–	1
Camping	9	G	6	1	1	1	–	1	–	2
		B	3	–	1	1	–	–	–	1
Gliding	9	G	2	–	1	1	–	–	–	–
		B	7	–	2	4	–	–	–	1
Parachuting	9	G	0	–	–	–	–	–	–	–
		B	9	–	4	3	–	–	–	2
Boxing	8	G	0	–	–	–	–	–	–	–
		B	8	–	2	1	–	–	–	5
Weight-lifting	8	G	1	–	–	–	–	–	–	1
		B	7	–	3	1	–	–	–	3
Wrestling	7	G	1	–	–	–	1	–	–	–
		B	6	–	1	–	1	–	–	4
Baseball	6	G	1	–	1	–	–	–	–	–
		B	5	–	2	–	–	–	–	3
Cross-country running	6	G	1	1	–	–	–	–	–	–
		B	5	1	–	–	–	–	1	3
Fishing	6	G	1	–	1	–	–	–	–	–
		B	5	–	–	3	–	–	–	2
Roller skating	6	G	6	1	3	2	–	–	–	–
		B	0	–	–	–	–	–	–	–
Flying	5	G	1	–	–	–	–	–	1	–
		B	4	–	1	2	–	–	–	1
Lacrosse	5	G	4	–	4	–	–	–	–	–
		B	1	–	1	–	–	–	–	–

	Total			Friends will not	Facilities far or lacking/no space	Expense/no equipment	Training lacking	Too young	Cannot get in a team/not good enough/physique	Other
Billiards	5	G	0	—	—	—	—	—	—	—
		B	5	—	2	3	—	—	—	—
Boating	4	G	3	—	2	—	—	—	—	1
		B	1	—	1	—	—	—	—	—
4/5 aside football	4	G	0	—	—	—	—	—	—	—
		B	4	—	4	—	—	—	—	—
Youth hostelling	4	G	4	—	—	1	—	1	—	2
		B	0	—	—	—	—	—	—	—
Dragster racing	4	G	1	—	1	—	—	—	—	—
		B	3	—	1	2	—	—	—	—
Croquet	2	G	2	—	1	1	—	—	—	—
		B	0	—	—	—	—	—	—	—
Dance-Educ.	2	G	2	—	1	—	—	—	—	1
		B	0	—	—	—	—	—	—	—
Keep-fit	2	G	2	—	1	—	—	—	—	1
		B	0	—	—	—	—	—	—	—
Rowing	2	G	1	—	1	—	—	—	—	—
		B	1	—	1	—	—	—	—	—
Ice hockey	2	G	0	—	—	—	—	—	—	—
		B	2	—	1	1	—	—	—	—
Outdoor Games	2	G	2	—	—	—	—	—	—	2
		B	0	—	—	—	—	—	—	—
Bowling (green)	1	G	0	—	—	—	—	—	—	—
		B	1	—	1	—	—	—	—	—
Mountaineering	1	G	0	—	—	—	—	—	—	—
		B	1	—	—	—	1	—	—	—
Water polo	1	G	0	—	—	—	—	—	—	—
		B	1	—	—	—	—	—	—	1
Stock car racing	1	G	0	—	—	—	—	—	—	—
		B	1	—	—	—	—	1	—	—
Skipping	1	G	1	—	—	—	—	—	—	1
		B	0	—	—	—	—	—	—	—
Darts	1	G	0	—	—	—	—	—	—	—
		B	1	—	1	—	—	—	—	—
Polo	1	G	0	—	—	—	—	—	—	—
		B	1	—	—	1	—	—	—	—
Cave diving	1	G	0	—	—	—	—	—	—	—
		B	1	—	—	—	—	—	—	1
Speed skating	1	G	1	—	1	—	—	—	—	—
		B	0	—	—	—	—	—	—	—

	Total		Friends will not	Facilities far or lacking/no space	Expense/no equipment	Training lacking	Too young	Cannot get in a team/not good enough/physique	Other
Bird Watching	1	G 0	—	—	—	—	—	—	—
		B 1	—	—	—	—	—	—	1
Fox hunting	1	G 0	—	—	—	—	—	—	—
		B 1	—	—	—	—	1	—	—
Diving	1	G 0	—	—	—	—	—	—	—
		B 1	—	—	—	—	—	—	1
Hot rod racing	1	G 0	—	—	—	—	—	—	—
		B 1	—	—	1	—	—	—	—
Falconry	1	G 0	—	—	—	—	—	—	—
		B 1	—	—	1	—	—	—	—
Shark fishing	1	G 0	—	—	—	—	—	—	—
		B 1	—	1	—	—	—	—	—
Bear hunting	1	G 0	—	—	—	—	—	—	—
		B 1	—	1	—	—	—	—	—
Bobsleigh	1	G 0	—	—	—	—	—	—	—
		B 1	—	1	—	—	—	—	—

TABLE 37

Individual activities which school leavers would do but do not, analysed by reasons given:
those who gave positive answers to this question from *secondary modern schools,* omitting
sports mentioned by fewer than fifteen children

	Total		Friends will not	Facilities far or lacking/no space	Expense/no equipment	Training lacking	Too young	Cannot get in a team/not good enough/physique	Other
Tennis	60	G 47	3	17	2	4	—	—	21
		B 13	1	3	2	—	—	1	6
Football	52	G 19	—	1	—	9	—	—	9
		B 33	3	4	1	3	—	4	18
Judo	48	G 28	1	8	1	5	1	—	12
		B 20	—	6	4	1	—	—	9
Ice skating	41	G 32	—	14	9	2	—	1	6
		B 9	—	4	3	—	—	—	2
Ten pin bowling	35	G 20	1	10	8	—	—	—	1
		B 15	—	8	6	—	—	—	1
Rugby	31	G 2	—	—	1	—	—	—	1
		B 29	4	7	—	3	1	—	14
Netball	29	G 29	2	11	—	2	—	—	14
		B 0	—	—	—	—	—	—	—
Swimming	29	G 18	2	1	1	1	—	—	13
		B 11	1	1	—	—	—	2	7
Badminton	22	G 7	—	5	1	—	—	—	1
		B 15	1	7	2	—	1	—	4
Basketball	20	G 4	1	—	—	—	—	1	2
		B 16	—	8	—	1	—	3	4
Athletics	19	G 6	—	3	—	1	—	—	2
		B 13	—	5	—	—	—	1	7
Cricket	19	G 5	1	—	—	1	—	—	3
		B 14	2	—	—	3	—	—	9
Horse riding	19	G 14	—	6	4	1	—	—	3
		B 5	—	1	3	1	—	—	—
Table tennis	19	G 9	—	4	2	—	—	—	3
		B 10	1	2	2	—	—	1	4
Golf	17	G 1	—	—	—	1	—	—	—
		B 16	—	2	8	2	—	—	4
Rounders	16	G 16	—	6	3	—	—	—	7
		B 0	—	—	—	—	—	—	—
Hockey	15	G 13	2	3	3	—	—	2	3
		B 2	—	—	1	—	—	—	1

TABLE 38
Individual activities which school leavers would do but do not, analysed by reasons given: those who gave positive answers to this question from *grammar and technical schools*, omitting sports mentioned by fewer than twelve children

	Total		Friends will not	Facilities far or lacking/no space	Expense/no equipment	Training lacking	Too young	Cannot get in a team/not good enough/physique	Other
Judo	50	G 22	2	4	5	—	1	—	10
		B 28	1	7	5	2	—	—	13
Ten pin bowling	46	G 32	2	14	12	—	—	—	4
		B 14	—	9	5	—	—	—	—
Golf	45	G 5	—	1	1	—	—	2	1
		B 40	—	6	20	1	—	—	13
Ski-ing	31	G 8	—	7	1	—	—	—	—
		B 23	—	16	7	—	—	—	—
Ice skating	28	G 25	1	13	9	—	—	—	2
		B 3	—	2	1	—	—	—	—
Canoeing	25	G 9	1	6	1	—	—	—	1
		B 16	—	9	5	—	—	—	2
Tennis	20	G 6	2	1	1	—	—	—	2
		B 14	2	3	2	—	—	—	7
Sailing	17	G 7	—	6	1	—	—	—	—
		B 10	—	3	6	—	—	—	1
Car racing/rallying	17	G 1	—	—	—	—	1	—	—
		B 16	—	—	15	—	1	—	—
Badminton	15	G 5	—	4	—	—	1	—	—
		B 10	—	8	—	—	—	—	2
Horse riding	15	G 13	1	3	7	—	—	—	2
		B 2	—	1	1	—	—	—	—
Rock climbing	14	G 4	—	3	1	—	—	—	—
		B 10	1	4	2	—	1	1	1
Football	13	G 1	1	—	—	—	—	—	—
		B 12	—	3	1	—	—	4	4
Aqualung	12	G 5	1	2	1	—	—	—	1
		B 7	—	5	2	—	—	—	—
Table tennis	12	G 4	—	3	—	—	—	—	1
		B 8	1	4	1	—	—	—	2

TABLE 39

Individual activities which school leavers would do but do not, analysed by reasons given: those who gave positive answers to this question from *direct grant schools,* omitting sports mentioned by fewer than five children

	Total			Friends will not	Facilities far or lacking/no space	Expense/no equipment	Training lacking	Too young	Cannot get in a team/not good enough/physique	Other
Golf	18	G	7	1	1	1	—	—	—	4
		B	11	—	—	4	—	—	1	6
Judo	17	G	10	—	4	2	—	—	—	4
		B	7	—	2	1	—	—	—	4
Tennis	17	G	3	1	—	—	—	—	—	2
		B	14	2	4	2	—	—	—	6
Sailing	10	G	8	1	3	3	—	—	—	1
		B	2	—	1	1	—	—	—	—
Badminton	9	G	4	—	3	—	—	—	—	1
		B	5	—	4	—	—	—	—	1
Horse riding	9	G	5	—	2	2	—	—	—	1
		B	4	—	1	3	—	—	—	—
Squash	8	G	2	—	2	—	—	—	—	—
		B	6	—	3	3	—	—	—	—
Canoeing	7	G	6	1	4	1	—	—	—	—
		B	1	—	—	1	—	—	—	—
Rock climbing	5	G	4	—	2	—	—	—	—	2
		B	1	—	—	—	—	—	—	1
Ski-ing	5	G	1	—	—	1	—	—	—	—
		B	4	—	2	2	—	—	—	—
Swimming	5	G	2	—	—	—	—	—	—	2
		B	3	—	—	—	2	—	—	1
Table tennis	5	G	1	—	1	—	—	—	—	—
		B	4	—	2	—	—	—	—	2
Ten pin bowling	5	G	2	—	2	—	—	—	—	—
		B	3	—	—	2	—	—	—	1

Index